ZEN : HAMANO & RYU

ZEN : HAMANO & RYU

CONTEMPORARY ART FROM JAPAN

10 August   7 September   1991

TALBOT   RICE   GALLERY
UNIVERSITY   OF   EDINBURGH

24 September   2 November   1991

NORTHERN   CENTRE   FOR
CONTEMPORARY ART, SUNDERLAND

THE   ARTS   CENTRE   WASHINGTON

THE JAPAN FESTIVAL 1991

SUPPORTED BY ———————————————————————

The Japan Foundation

The Kagawa Foundation

THE SPONSORSHIP OF THIS EXHIBITION BY NINE OF THE
PARTICIPATING COMPANIES HAS BEEN RECOGNISED BY AN AWARD
UNDER THE GOVERNMENT'S BUSINESS SPONSORSHIP INCENTIVE
SCHEME, WHICH IS ADMINISTERED BY THE ASSOCIATION FOR
BUSINESS SPONSORSHIP OF THE ARTS.

Subsidised by the Scottish Λrts Council

THIS EXCITING EXHIBITION of contemporary Japanese art, taking place in Edinburgh and Sunderland, offers the Japanese business community a prime opportunity to demonstrate our commitment and support in two such important locations.

Twenty Japanese companies have participated in this joint sponsorship of the Hamano exhibition and we are all proud to be associated in this way with the Japan Festival 1991.

The aims of the Festival include the desire to create better understanding between the British and Japanese peoples through cultural exchange.

We believe that this exhibition will help to achieve that goal by giving visitors the opportunity to enjoy the works of Toshihiro Hamano and his group.

SHINJI YATSUZUKA   **KEIICHI SHIMAKURA**

Mitsubishi Electric UK Limited   NEC Semiconductors (UK) Limited

Members of the Scottish Committee of The Japan Festival

SPONSORS

Alps Electric (UK) Ltd.

CANON SCOTLAND
BUSINESS MACHINES LTD.

COMMITTED TO TOTAL QUALITY

 Eadie Bros & Co Limited

    Japan Airlines

 JVC Manufacturing UK Ltd.

 MITSUBISHI

 MIZUNO (UK) LIMITED

 NEC Semiconductors (UK) Ltd.

 OKI UK Limited

 The Sanwa Bank Limited

 Shin-Etsu Handotai Europa Ltd.

SII
Seiko Instruments U.K. Ltd.

 SUMITRUST IVORY & SIME LTD

 TENMA

 YKK (U.K.) LTD.

WITH DONATIONS FROM

Kibun Co (UK) Ltd, Tamura Hinchley Ltd, Kintetsu World Express (UK) Ltd and Jascot Travel Ltd.

Introduction

The Japan Festival 1991 has as its patrons H.R.H. The Prince of Wales and H.I.H. The Crown Prince of Japan. The Festival is being held throughout Great Britain and I sincerely believe that it will be greatly significant in the promotion of goodwill and friendship between our two nations.

As Chairman of the Scottish Committee of the Japan Festival I am delighted that this important exhibition; 'Zen: Hamano and Ryu', will open in Edinburgh, subsequently touring to Sunderland.

This collection of contemporary art by Toshihiro Hamano and his pupils has successfully toured Europe in recent years and the quality and creativity of their work is highly regarded. I am confident that British visitors to the exhibition will be enlightened and stimulated.

The exhibition has been generously supported by the administrative governments of Kagawa Prefecture and Sakaide Town and sponsored in the United Kingdom by twenty Japanese companies operating in Scotland. This significant financial support from different parts of the world illustrates the cultural partnership which is one of the principal objectives of the Japan Festival.

My thanks and commendation to all those involved in the creation of this beautiful exhibition, which I hope will forge an even stronger link between Great Britain and Japan.

George Younger, T.D., D.L., M.P.
Chairman
Scottish Committee, Japan Festival 1991

Message

Japan Festival 1991, a project to introduce Japan in commemoration of the 100th anniversary of the establishment of the Japan Society, is held in various places in the UK with the cooperation of the British and Japanese governments as well as private organizations in both countries.

The contemporary art exhibition, "Zen: Hamano & Ryu" originated from an exchange between people from the UK and Japan, and has been realized following the recommendation of the British Committee. It is my great pleasure to see this exhibition held in the UK, offering an extremely significant opportunity for cultural exchange between the two countries.

It goes without saying that how well Japan and the East are understood in Western society is very important. Recently the trend to discover the essence of Zen philosophy has been revived in Western society. The works by Mr Hamano, who is now attracting a great deal of attention, reflect his appreciation of Oriental philosophy and will give inspiration to Western art in the future.

I would like to express my respect for the tireless efforts made by all the people concerned in organizing this exhibition and hope that its success will provide momentum for further cultural exchange between the UK and Japan.

Seiichiro Otsuka
Consul General of Japan in Edinburgh

Message

I should like to offer my congratulations to Toshihiro Hamano on the opening of his "Zen: Hamano & Ryu" in the Japan Festival 1991.

Kagawa Prefecture, where Toshihiro Hamano has made his home, is a area blessed with the splendour of nature. To the north is the magnificence of the Seto Inland Sea, while to the south is the grandeur of the Asan mountain range. As well as an abundance of produce, this land has given birth to countless cultural achievements. In particular, those of the great religious leader of the eighth century, Kobo Daishi (Kukai), who was the first great philosopher to advocate cultural exchanges between East and West (China).

Although the era is vastly different, it is in such a land that Toshihiro Hamano has established the *Ryu* group with the aim of expanding the artistic culture of our region both throughout Japan and overseas. And as one of the key programmes of the Japan Festival, "Zen: Hamano & Ryu" will open in Edinburgh and Sunderland on the recommendation of the British Festival Committee, and for this Toshihiro Hamano must be heartily congratulated.

I am confident that, as an exhibition with a vision that reaches into the future, and also as a stage for artists of tomorrow, "Zen: Hamano & Ryu" will cross national boundaries to open in all parts of the world, while remaining attuned to the times through its great diversity.

I should like to wish great success for the Festival, and good health and prosperity of all members of the committees from both Japan and the United Kingdom.

Joichi Hirai
Governor, Kagawa Prefecture
Chairman, Kagawa Foundation.

Message

Congratulations on the opening of the "Zen: Hamano & Ryu" exhibition.

Contemporary Art *Ryu* was established in Sakaide City in March 1971 by Toshihiro Hamano, and in the twenty years since then has been very active in the international world of art.

Ryu, comprising Toshihiro Hamano and his pupils, have carved out and brought to realisation their own art world by developing a creative fusion of East and West, and their international artistic achivements in Yugoslavia, Austria, Germany and many other countries have been highly acclaimed.

Sakaide City can take great pride in *Ryu*'s selection as the representative for the contemporary art exhibition that forms a part of the Japan Festival 1991, a grand presentation of Japanese culture that will head to all parts of the United Kingdom, and we all wish them great success.

The Exhibition will be held in the Talbot Rice Gallery, Old College, University of Edinburgh, and in June the curator of the *gallery*, Dr Duncan Macmillan, visited Japan in preparation for the exhibition. During his stay I had the opportunity to hold very fruitful discussions with him regarding cultural exchages between Edinburgh and Sakaide.

An international profile and a strong appreciation for culture are extremely important to the development of regional society. As *Ryu* soars to even greater heights in their quest for universal beauty, I am sure that their achievements will have a direct bearing on the creation and elevation of regional culture, and will make a significant contribution to the further expansion of cultural relations between Sakaide and the two cities of Edinburgh and Sunderland, and also between the United Kingdom and Japan.

Toshiaki Matsuura
Mayor, Sakaide City

Greetings

Spiritual enlightenment is achieved by "nothingness" of Zen. "Nothingness" is a teaching to emancipate oneself and give up everything. Master Dogen said, "To learn self is to forget self, and to forget self means that true self is Identified in the universe. "He taught the way the nature and human beings are to be, and I presume his words are interpreted in the world of art to mean separation from the nature in everyday-life, and to transcend the separation and get back to it as a completely new being. It is to realize that inconvenience (what is perceived from relative opposing concepts) is freedom. It is to be the nature itself. We have to recognize the essence that, by getting at the root of the Oriental and the Occidental notions, i.e. "nothingness" of Zen and "wisdom" in the West and by contemplating them from the modern viewpoint, the basis to pursue a new way will be created.

In the late 1960s I keenly felt that a "real" artist can be grown only through communion of soul, and established *Ryu* in 1971. Since then, beyond personal activities as an artist, I have collaborated with young artists to try to change the mechanism and common ideas of the society which surrounds the world of art. I have come to realise through the experiences of global exchage which we have promoted in the past decade that the vistas of the future of art will be opened up by probing deep into the Oriental and the Occidental culture.

It is our greatest honur to be given this opportunity to participate in the modern art exhibition of Japan Festival 1991 which introduces Japanese culture in the twentieth year of the establishment of *Ryu* . It must be mentioned that we fully appreciate Talbot Rice Gallery, University of Edinburgh and Northern Centre for Contemporary Art.
Suderland, The Arts centre, Washington the sponsors, the committee members both in the UK and Japan, generous cooperation for this exhibition rendered by Mr. Joe Earl and Mr. Duncan Macmillan, and Mrs. Jackie McGlone who travelled all the way to Japan to write about us. Our hearty gratitude is also extended to the governmental organizations in UK and Japan, the Japan Foundation, the Kagawa Foundation, Sakaide City government, the Japanese companies in UK and the press in both countries for their kind cooperation and support.

Toshihiro Hamano
Leader, Ryu Contemporary Art

Contents

17- **Toshihiro Hamano : Modern Art and the Art of Zen**
Duncan Macmillan

23- **Toshihiro Hamano**

**About the Phases of Art :
Conversation with Hideo Mineshima**

The Worlds of Art Harmonise
Toshihiro Hamano

Being between East and West
Toshihiro Hamano

The Spirit of the Ryu Group
Curt Heigl

Between Wind and Storm
Zoran Kržišnik

Hamano and Ljubljana
Jure Mikuž

Comments
Hajime Nakamura
Ichiro   Fukuzawa
Yoichiro Omachi

41- **Biographies of Toshihiro Hamano**

48- **List of Works**

51- **Catalogue of Works by Toshihiro Hamano**

109- **Ryu : Members of Ryu**

111- **History of Ryu**

115- **Catalogue of Works by Members of Ryu**

Toshihiro Hamano: Modern Art and the Art of Zen

For many years, Toshihiro Hamano has been a student of Zen Buddhism and, although Shintoism is the offcial religion of Japan, Zen has had a central influence on the whole of Japanese life: "Zen has entered internally into every phase of the cultural life of the people."(1) In giving contemporary expression to the ideas of Zen therefore, Hamano is seeking to reaffirm a system of values which is close to the heart of Japanese culture. This is the motive behind his painting in this exhibition and although in its scale, its simplicity and the apparently non-figurative form of its imagery, it relates visibly to Western abstract art, this motive distinguishes it. It is in part a superficial resemblance, too, for these pictures are not wholly abstract. They are meditative images based on motifs derived from the religious architecture of ancient Japan.

These marvellous temples and pagodas, many dating from the eighth and ninth centuries, are built of wood and in their architecture, space and structure interpenetrate in a way that is very different from the Western tradition. In it, space is defined by drawing a contrast between mass and void. Leaving aside the Gothic, in the West, space is generally opposed to structure, therefore, and is enclosed by it. Even the largest of these Japanese buildings, however, the great, horned temple of Daibutsu-den in Nara, for instance, which is the largest wooden building in the world, does not enclose a simple, dramatic space as a Western building of similar size would usually do. Imitating this Japanese style, Mackintosh recreated its kind of space brilliantly in the library of Glasgow School of Art. It is an architecture in which space is inherent in structure and is not separately defined. Instead, extraordinary complexity and richness is achieved by a visible structure that is based on the lines and intersections in space of the wooden beams.
These intersections sometimes involve corbelling as many as five or six joints up and outwards

in a series to create the angle of a great, flying roof, or to join the tiers of beams that subdivide the volume of an internal space. The practical logic of this system is seen in the survival of some of these great buildings for more than a thousand years in an earthquake zone, but they are also endowed with complex symbolism. The pagoda for instance, with its five levels of roof and its towering golden spire, is not a building which contains a function as something conceptually separate. It is a symbolic structure; *being* is its function.(Fig.1)

Fig.1   Five-storied pagoda, Horyu-ji Temple, '7th c.

In Hamano's pictures, structure and space are integrated in just the same way as they are in this temple architecture and with a similar, though less specific, symbolic function. The black line of his compositions performs the same function as the wooden beams whose forms it reflects. In the earlier works, it

17

has a triangular section, the shape of the cross-section of the beams in some of the early Buddhist structures in Japan. This triangular section gives a sinuous complexity to Hamano's line. As it moves in the picture space, its profile changes naturally as it would do, seen from our viewpoint. Thus we appreciate clearly its movement. Recently, this line in the paintings has taken on a rectangular section, but the shapes in the paintings of this kind always echo the structures themselves; the three-part Phoenix Hall of the eleventh-century Byodo-in Temple, for instance, the rising tiers of a pagoda, or the plain interior of a teahouse.

These are not in any simple sense architectural paintings, but nor on the other hand do they belong to the traditional iconography of Zen art. In fact, most of the buildings that inspire them predate the introduction of Zen Buddhism into Japan which did not happen till the twelfth century. The traditonal art of Zen is a kind of *arte povero* though; austere, reduced and simple, and in that sense these pictures do belong squarely within this tradition. Reflecting this economy of means, Hamano for some years now has used only black and white, and their combination, grey. Black he says, too, is *gen*, a word which translates not only as black, but also as 'disinterestedness'.

This is a characteristic Zen concept, though its use in painting here is also akin to Mondrian's reduction of colour to the essential minimum, though it is even more severe. As Hamano uses black and white, he achieves the complete elimination of sentimentality and of anything extraneous. Thus he provides an equivalent to the symbolic structures of the buildings that are his inspiration. The pagoda for instance, as it rises through its stages, has at its centre a single column on which the whole structure depends. In the series of three meditative pictures, this central column can clearly be seen as the matrix of the composition, but in the pagoda itself, as this column rises up through the different levels, it serves a symbolic purpose. It unites them, but, usually decorated with *Mandalas,* it is also expressive of the aspiration of the spirit and

this is how Hamano sees it in his painting. It is this aspiration that leads the composition through its successive stages of simplification towards the ultimate, Zen state of 'Emptiness' in which the dualistic distinction between experience and the thing experienced disappears.

In these paintings, in his pursuit of Emptiness, in spite of their structural and architectural inspiration, Hamano deliberately negates the perspective of his forms. The projection of a shape is cancelled as its curve returns to the picture plane, or the logic of perspective is contradicted by a line that denies recession. His structures therefore, although they are spatially dynamic, do not assume a separate, spatial existence from the ground of the painting. This of course can be seen as a post-cubist device, but Hugo van der Goes had used it in the *Trinity College Altarpiece* in the late fifteenth century just as Hamano does now and both artists use it for a very different purpose to that proposed by the cubist tradition. In the outer panels of that painting, van der Goes contrasts the temporal space occupied by Edward Bonkil, the donor, on the right, with the space in the vision of the Trinity in the left-hand panel that is the object of his contemplation. In this panel, the rules of structure and perspective are denied. We can see with Bonkil, therefore, that his vision is spiritual. What he is seeing is taking place in a space in which the rules of mundane, temporal reality do not prevail.

Hamano creates a similar kind of mental space, but it also has a further spiritual dimension which relates specifically to Zen. The lack of opposition between space and void, and their interpenetration, as it is seen in the buildings which are the inspiration of his motifs, invokes a principle which is fundamental to the spirit of that philosophy. At the heart of Zen and analogous to Emptiness is the idea of 'Transparency'. This is the elimination of the distinction between subject and object and expresses the idea of a singleness that embraces all nature. Contrasting West and East in this, Daisetz Suzuki, the Japanese sage who did more than any other to introduce the ideas of Zen to the

West, wrote:

If the Greeks taught us how to reason and Christianity what to believe, it is Zen that teaches us to go beyond logic⋯ The Zen point of view is to find an absolute point where no dualism in whatever form obtains. Logic starts from the division of subject and object, and belief distinguishes between what is seen and what is not seen. The Western mode of thinking can never do away with this eternal dilemma, this or that, reason or faith, Man or God. With Zen all these are swept aside as something veiling our insight into the nature of life and reality. (2)

The same idea from a different perspective is reflected in the recent series of paintings that Hamano has done on the theme of the teahouse. The tea-ceremony and the teahouses built for it, together express something that is central to the Zen tradition. The ancient teahouses, like the Taian teahouse built by Sen-no-Rikyu, the sixteenth-century master of the tea-ceremony, are small, simple, even deliberately primitive Buildings and in that respect are very much in contrast to the splendours of traditional Buddhist architecture,

Fig.2   Interior of Taian teahouse, Myokian Temple by Sen no Rikyu, 16th c.

but they are also open to the space that surrounds them in a way that reflects the same basic idea, the elimination of duality. This is the first thing that one feels in Hamano's teahouse series, the spatial openness of the structure, and in the teahouse this interpenetration of internal and external space is crucial to the significance of the whole ritual. Takuan, a sixteenth-century abbot, wrote of 'cha-no-yu', the ethos of the tea-ceremony: (Fig.2)

The principle of the tea ceremony is the spirit of harmonious blending of Heaven and Earth ... Let us then construct a small room in a bamboo grove or under trees, arrange streams and rocks and plant trees and bushes, while inside let us pile up charcoal, set a kettle, arrange flowers, and arrange in order the necessary tea utensils. And let all this be carried out in accordance with the idea that in this room we can enjoy the streams and rocks as we do the rivers and mountains in Nature.(3)

A perfect example of this is the seventeenth-century teahouse in the garden at the Toji-in temple in Kyoto. The small, thatched teahouse stands above and is open to the beautiful landscape garden of trees, rocks and water. The naturalness of the ceremony reflects the naturalness of the garden and so they become one.

The spirituality of the tea-ceremony lies in its ordinariness. This was in its origin perhaps also true of the bread and wine in the Christian sacrament of Communion, but this was always a means to something else, a stepping stone from the ordinary to the transcendental. It is not an end in itself therefore, but that is precisely the essential characteristic of Zen; the thing in itself, the approach to the 'isness' of things and the intuitive apprehension of their essence. Suzuki summed it up in a phrase: "what is, is — which is the final act of experience."(4)

This, the Zen absolute, is expressed most lucidly in the unique Japanese gardens of rocks and sand. The most famous of these is the garden of Ryoan-ji in Kyoto. It is composed of fifteen rocks in a field of white sand, or marble chippings, raked into parallel lines, except round the rocks where it breaks into concentric circles. This is the Zen art form to which Hamano's painting is closest. It is austere, but far from simple. The rocks become incidents or events. They vibrate within their concentric circles and the whole field is made dynamic by the raked lines. It could be either time or space. It is certainly not neutral. The black figure and the white ground in Hamano's painting work in just the same way.

This is not a casual comparison, for the artist has actually created a Zen rock-garden himself at the Sanjoso restaurant in Takamatsu. This work is typical of him, but it is also and more generally typical of the way in which Zen still informs Japanese culture, for a rock garden of this kind in a restaurant is not just a piece of fashionable decor. The spiritual beauty of the garden is carried through the whole in a way that is almost inconceivable in the West. Every aspect of the restaurant, from the decor of the rooms, also designed by the artist, to the presentation of the food, is controlled by the same aesthetic sense because it reflects the same fundamental philosophy; the philosophy that is epitomised in the tea-ceremony and which is also expressed in the beautiful formality of Japanese manners. It was this unity of sensibility in Japan which captivated Western artists a hundred years ago, and at the same time they found inspiration for a new kind of spirituality in the more abstract approach of Japanese art. The question of whether or not this tradition can survive, now, in a technological age and under the assault of Western ideas is part of what has prompted Hamano to make such an energetic restatement of this Japanese tradition.

This interpenetration of art and life is also another aspect of Zen unity and it is reflected elsewhere in Hamano's work, too. He has not limited his function as an artist to the stark black and white canvases which are the main part of the current exhibition. The social dimension of his art is very important to him. On the one hand, as well as the Sanjoso restaurant, his public works include a ceiling painting in the Sakaide Kannonji temple, a large and important *Mandala* of the Buddha with the eight virtues and the four seasons, all defended by a dragon in a second ceiling in the entrance porch of the temple. He also has another major commission of a similar kind for a new temple in Nara, the first great centre of Japanese Buddhism in the eighth century, and he has executed a major public work of a different kind in a commission for the gymnasium of Sakaide. It is a painting eight metres long and in a single line it epitomises the movement of the gymnast. (Fig.3)

Fig.3   Ceiling Painting Mandala, Sakaide Kannon-ji Temple, by Toshihiro Hamano,1982

In addition though, Hamano is a celebrated teacher who has inspired devotion in his pupils. He is the founder of *Ryu*, a vigorous organization of artists. It has seventy members, a number of whom are showing along with him here. Most of the members of *Ryu* are his pupils, but *Ryu* has in turn also created an art academy which it seems likely will soon become publicly established. Hamano has founded this group in the town of Sakaide, a salt-producing and ship-building town, otherwise mostly famous only for the Seto Ohashi bridge, the world's longest, which joins the island of Shikoku with the mainland across the inland Sea. By choosing Sakaide, rather than joining the fashionable art world of Tokyo, Hamano has taken an important, public initiative. It has also been a very successful one. Sakaide does not have a previous cultural tradition, but by his energy and example, he has generated remarkable support for the visual arts in the city and in its neighbour, Takamatsu. This has come from among the community and especially from the leaders of local government. Thus he has further demonstrated the immediate engagement of his art and this is true to the Zen tradition:

> Reality or Suchness or Emptiness is taken hold of in the midst of the concrete living facts of the universe, and not abstracted from them by means of thought. Zen never leaves this world of facts.(5)

Zen is not a mystical religion set apart from life, therefore, and because of its character, some of the most distinctive values of Japanese secular society are religious in origin. Even such central Western ideas as freedom and the individual, like their Japanese equivalents were also religious in origin, however, though now they are irrecoverably secularised and, inseparable from politics, have lost touch with their roots. It was for freedom of conscience in matters of belief — and nowhere more than in Scotlando — that the West's greatest ideological battles were fought. Nevertheless, in contrast to Zen, Western thought, as it has become secularised seems also to have become irreducibly dualistic. It depends on object and subject, whether it is God and Man, the scientist and his experiment, or the artist and his model.

The motives that have produced Western abstract art, in which by definition there is no model — no 'other' — are various. They range from those of Mondrian and Malevich to Jackson Pollock or Alan Davie, but common among them has been the search for a way to overcome this dualism and in the twentieth century, artists in the West have frequently turned to the unity of Zen for guidance in this. It has therefore played a significant role in the whole evolution of abstract art, but the predisposition to favour intuitive simplicity in painting and to reject the more elaborate kinds of constructed, pictorial reflection of the observed world — the idea

that mind and hand work better together if the intellect does not come between them — has its roots much earlier in the history of Western thought.

At the centre of the development of modern art there have been two key ideas, the supremacy of the imagination among the human faculties, originally as the agent of sympathy, the key to moral feeling; and the idea that knowledge of the world is acquired intuitively, that therefore the cultivation of the intellect as a separate faculty may actually be a hindrance to the acquisition of true understanding of the nature of reality. This approach is seen in the art of the Surrealists and especially of Miró, perhaps through the influence of Georges Duthuit, an early interpreter of Zen. It is also seen in the work of a number of the American abstract expressionists, and closer to home, in that of William Johnstone and Alan Davie. Unconsciously though, these artists were perhaps all reflecting a much longer convergence of thought between East and West which is at the centre of the development of modern art, but whose real significance has been lost from sight, much as Hamano now fears the values of Zen may be lost from sight in Japan.

Already in the eighteenth century, William Blake attacked the dualism of Western thought in terms of the division that he saw between reason and imagination, upholding the superiority of imaginative or intuitive over rational or deductive knowledge — knowledge supported by intellect. Before Blake, these ideas had found their first formulation here in Scotland, where David Hume's account of human nature and especially Thomas Reid's intuitive theory of perception were allied to the theory of moral sympathy expounded by Adam Smith. According to Smith, following Hume, the agent of moral understanding is sympathy, a function of feeling which is intuitive, not subject to intellectual control and the province of the imagination. The cultivation of the free imagination was therefore originally a moral priority.

Intuition is of course also central to Zen

philosophy. In realising the Zen objective of the understanding of the nature of reality;

> The clearing away of all conceptual scaffolds is imperative. When Zen speaks of transparency, it means this clearing away, this thorough wiping of the surface of the mind-mirror.(6)

The Western idea of intuition is certainly not to be confused with the teaching of Zen, but there are remarkable analogies too. It was, for example, this alliance of the intuitive theory of perception with the theory of the moral role of the imagination which led in the eighteenth century in the West (and again first in Scotland) to the emulation of primitive art, seen as the expression of pure, imaginative perception, unobscured by the ponderous, 'conceptual scaffolding' of generations of learned response. This has a precise parallel with Zen. The Zen tea-house as established by Rikyu, for example, is almost identical with the eighteenth-century paradigm of the Adam primitive, Adam's Hut, the first house as built it in Paradise. The analogy with the Western, primitve nature tradition that runs from Rousseau to Thoreau and beyond, is clear.

The original objective of the cleansing and cultivation of the imagination, as we have seen, was moral. This objective was to find the universal in the individual, to find what it is that in a state of innocence, we would all share without barrier. This is the basis of the idea of moral sympathy and in this form it bears a distinct resemblance to the Zen idea of 'transparency', though in a moral, rather than a purely existential universe. In trying to reach this and to dispose of the 'otherness' of painting, however, artists have inevitably slipped into solepsism. Under the relentless pressure of Western dualism, if there is no 'other', then there is only self. It is here that the Modernist tradition has again diverged radically from Zen. In the role that it has given to self, Western art followed Nietzsche.

Thus, in spite of those who stood for somethig different, as Modernism developed, self was elevated into the object of art and as this has happened, so the modern tradition has been separated from the moral base with which it originated. The cleansing of the imagination by turning to nature and the intuitive simplicity of primitive art was in its origin a means of securing a new clarity of moral perception, but in seeking this, we have been left instead with the sterile idea of art as self-expression. Zen, on the other hand, suggests a very different idea and one that might also help us to understand once again our own tradition:

> The aesthetic aspect of Zen teaching is closely related to Zen asceticism in that there is in both the absence of self-hood, the merging of subject and object in one absolute emptiness.(7)

Hamano's work is purely Japanese, but it has both a universal relevance therefore and a special topicality, for the reaction against this solepsism in the Modernist tradition and the restatement of a wider system of values is the motivation of much of the most serious art of Post-modernism. Ironically, at just the moment that Nietzsche was putting forward the argument for the supremacy of the individual will, in the Arts and Crafts movement, Walter Crane was arguing with passion a very different view, that the artist should be anonymous, transparent even. This has remained an alternative, if submerged, tradition in the West, but it was seen for instance in the art of Miró, of all Western artists of his generation, the one closest to Zen and the most admired in Japan. The Zen model that Hamano offers us is therefore something that we can share and that is profoundly relevant to the contemporary dilemma of Western art.

Duncan Macmillan
Curator, Talbot Rice Gallery

NOTES: 1.Daisetz T.Suzuki, *Zen and Japanese Culture*, (Tokyo 1988) p21 2.Suzuki, *Zen*,p360 3.Quoted, Suzuki, *Zen*, p276 4.Suzuki, *Zen*, p34 5.Suzuki, *Zen*, p347 6.Suzuki, *Zen*, p360 7.Suzuki, *Zen*, p352

Toshihiro Hamano

Fig.4   Toshihiro Hamano in his Atelier

About the Phases of Art
Extract from *Geijutsu no Iso wo Kataru* -Conversation with Dr Hideo Mineshima-

Art and Religion

Mineshima: To begin with, I'd like to discuss the issue of whether art and paintings belong to the individual, In the case of religion, there is an understanding that it is an issue of whether one will be saved or not, and is entirely up to the individual, although it has nothing to do with egoism.

Hamano: I think art is slightly different from religion. Perhaps universality is the right word, but I believe that art takes hold in an area "detached from the individual", in the sense that to society it has an appeal that reaches beyond the individual.

I have the feeling that art is, -if anything- relative, and I believe that the interesting aspect of art is that these two concepts are partly connected, and from these connected areas they branch off, only to be reconnected at some other point.

Mineshima: The two concepts you mentioned just now are the absolute concept and the relative concept, aren't they. Could you be a little more specific.?

Hamano: Taking the image of Buddha as an example, we can see that the image itself is viewed as an object of religion, that is, an object of faith, but on the other hand, it can also be viewed as an object of beauty.

Mineshima: Don't you think there is something in art that comes close to faith.?

Hamano: Although totally different, they are connected in certain areas. In the process of their becoming connected at some area, an artist, becomes absolute and draws nearer to religion during the process of producing the "object". Here spiritual enlightenment is achieved, and from here the artist moves on to the next step where spiritual enlightenment is again achieved. In art we commonly refer to this as "development".

Development is very important to the artist. This is so not only in art, but also in *Noh* and fields not directly related to art, like dancing.

It may not be called "development", but it is, nevertheless, a carving out of new paths.

When an artist achieves development it is not outwardly discernible, but there is something inside -depth- that does not exist on the surface. It is at this stage that an artist draws nearer to religion.

Mineshima: In this sense, it is an absolute concept, isn't it.

Hamano: For example, in art there is a point at which the painter must take the brush from the canvas. In dance or *Noh*, the position and movement of hands and legs of course express the inner being, but the point at which the movement stops suddenly, known as the "cut", is critical. It is the timing of this cut that determines whether a piece of work is of high quality, or whether a dance leaves a lasting impression.

My work is abstract, somewhat similar to calligraphy, and for me how I incorporate the "cut", into my work at the beginning and the end is absolutely crucial; for example, Should the "cut" be vertical or horizontal? Should it be curved or straight? Or should there be a series of cuts all over the work.

Mineshima: The German philosopher Hegel talks of this in terms of becoming and ceasing to be, and in Hegel's concept of dialectics, the beginning is the end, the end is the beginning. Here the beginning is different from the very first beginning. If we put it this way, in a certain sense, the question of how to end a "cut" is also a question of how to begin a "cut".

Art and Nature

Mineshima: Nature is not something that we have created, whereas art is something that we humans can create.

However, there are aspects in which nature and art share common ground. Nature is, as indicated in the statement "nature - the great artist" (German philosopher Emmanuel Kant), is created in exactly the same manner as art. In contrast, art is "genius art" (Kant's words), and if genius is nothing more than a gift of nature, nature and art are not opposing concepts, and I believe that artists have much to learn from nature.

Hamano: Yes, there is much to learn from nature, and nature has much to teach us. It is important that people who are producing or intend to produce an abstract painting observe nature again, even more intently.

Mineshima: So there is a backbone of body and substance, rather than creating away on concept alone.

Hamano: In both cases of proceeding with an abstract idea and painting while looking at the object, oneself is, after all, the core. But since there are limits in human life, if we pursue something seriously or with all our heart, we may come to know ourselves and our capacities. Then, if we proceed to a certain stage and attempt to tackle it even more earnestly, nature will teach us as a matter of course.

It isn't that nature teaches us through a clear voice, or through clear images; instead we realise it all of a sudden, it is like an instantaneous flash of inspiration.

Mineshima: We human beings are living within the confines of time and space. So I believe that art or creation is also executed within the same confines. Two words that you use regularly, time (jikan) and space (kukan), contain the word *ma* (an alternative reading for the kan character; this has both time and space meanings). Could you explain this a little, please.

Hamano: The concept of *ma* has been discussed at length throughout the history of Japanese art, so there is no great need to repeat what has already been said, but I believe that this very period, when there is about ten years left in the present century, is extremely important.

Mineshima: Is the *ma* of time and space the period (aida; another reading for the kan/ ma character) between time and space? Or is it that time is time, and *ma* represents the

time leading up to the 21st century?

Hamano: It has both meanings, but I believe while there is the question of *ma* in the broad sense, there are much more focused *ma* for individual cases, but normally *ma* is momentary *ma*.

In music, *ma* is a rest, a period of no sound. On paper, it is the blank paper, an area of no writing. In the West, this period of no sound is taken as a condition in which there is absolutely no sound to be heard, and this area of no writing is taken as a vacant space where nothing is to be written. But in Japan, people have a presentiment of signs, sounds or change in *ma*. However I cannot speak too generally, for people in the West have recently started to understand this concept.

Mineshima: After all, we humans are confined by time and space, and it is because we are confined that we will, conversely speaking, overcome this confinement.

Your comments in the book of your paintings mention the word "overcome", but doesn't it mean that, in a sense, for artistic activities it is always necessary to "overcome" And you mentioned that artists are people who create unknown value, and I believe that this was a different way of expressing "overcome". In such a sense, we humans are, time-wise, clinging to the past, and space wise, settled in regional society. And this we must "overcome". However, I believe that simply to "overcome" is of little use. Unless we "overcome", and then effectuate it again within time and space, there is no reality, and conversely, an abstract object cannot be created.

The book of your paintings contains a section on the "Social Nature of Art", in which you mention that artists should come to grips with the issue of art and society, but as touched on earlier, this is related to the question of whether art belongs to the individual. You have organised a contemporary art group known as *Ryu* in Sakaide, Shikoku, as a part of your arts campaign. I believe the reason behind the establishment of *Ryu* is that in production the individual has limits, but these limits of the individual can be surmounted when production is performed by a group, But what I should like to ask you is what are the limits of art production performed by the individual? And, what kinds of effects are there when it is performed by the group?

Hamano: Art is an individual performance, and in modern times, people have been painting and creating for themselves. At this point, there is no way that we can escape from egoistic attachment. In that case, we can say that when the artist's life comes to an end, so too does his or her work. In a sense, the artist's creative activities come to an end. But if there are people who appreciate the artist's work, then it does not end with the artist 's death. I believe we can say this is the continuation of non-continuation, This is what I refer to as "unopened".

Mineshima: So the opposite of what we call "open" is "closed". That concept is one of " closed society" and " open society", expressions often used by the French philosopher Henri-Louis Bergson."Closed society refers to one particular place, whereas open society concerns the whole of humanity. "Open ethics" are, in short, a love for humankind. This also applies to religion. Europeans are Christians, so to them "closed religions"–Judaism, Hinduism, Shintoism, in fact any of the non–Christian religions — are religions of nothing but "empty space". In contrast,"open religion" is a religion of love, in short, Christianity. This is a distinction that applies in the Christian world.

I believe that it can be looked at in this way, but the expressions "closed" and "open" can be applied to various areas, and as you just mentioned, I suppose art production by the individual is, in a sense, closed.

Hamano: Yes, I think it is closed. Artists have space that confines them to the studio. In Buddhism, this is priests' putting all their effort into their practice of asceticism, and the power to open will depend on how ascetic the priest is in his ascetic practices. Even if artists do not confine themselves to the studio, living and painting within life are not separate; the point is how their view of life is expressed directly through their actions.

Mineshima: In the case of the group, if anything it is "open". In a sense, the secret of your production lies here, and this will be passed on to your students. Does this mean that you no longer exist as an individual?

Hamano: Yes, that's right. In the spirit of a self-renunciation in which the individial ceases to exist, it is important that human beings be mentally prepared for recapture and improvement while maintaining a constant distance. For example, this is expressed in the beauty of the flowing lines that can be seen in the bodhisattva bust in Chuguji Temple or the Buddhist image door painting kept in the Tamamushi Shrine in the Horyuji Temple. We can come to life as a new being only once we have discarded ourselves. I believe that the world of creation will be with" purity "and " neatness ".

Mineshima: Therefore, when we in the academic world carry out research within, say, a learned society group, we naturally work hard together, and here it does not become a "closed society", rather, it becomes an "open society" in the fine sense. I believe that things an individual cannot do can be done by a group that is working hard together.

Hamano: When we attempt to open up ourselves, there are naturally parts that we cannot open alone, so we dash this against society. Hence artists may appear to have anti-Establishment tendencies. The tradition that comes with a fight is important for the avant-garde artists, and tradition is something that must be seized through constant hardship.

For example, I sometimes paint something like metallic light. This is not merely the light of an object, there is something much more spiritual in there.

Mineshima: For example, you used colour for your painting of the Mandala flower. And for your recent constructive abstract paintings, which bear a slight resemblance to calligraphy, you did not use colour. You have developed in this way, but from our view, if there are limits in using colour, you can simply

Fig.5 Dry landscape garden, Sanuki Sanjo-so, by Toshihiro Hamano, 1990

Hamano: All white is no good. White itself is important, but completely white is of no use, so we must put some kind of mark. But when making a mark, the area of white and the area of the mark must be perfectly harmonised, otherwise there is no point whatsoever in making the mark in the first place.

Mineshima: The following episode involving the 16th century tea master Sen no Rikyu is very well known. Rikyu came to a place that had just been cleaned by his students. Their cleaning was perfect, for the ground was spotless. It was, so to speak, "completely white". But around there Rikyu scattered a few leaves. Like the brush stroke you just mentioned, isn't it?

Even when colour is discarded from paintings, although we say they are without colour, they are in black and white, aren't they. So afer all, colour does in fact remain. This, I suppose, is art.

Hamano: The 16th/17th century Buddhist priest Takuan Soho wrote in his famous "*Fudo Chishin Myoroku*" (Ineffable Art of Calmness) that when we do anything, if our hearts stop at the doing action, our efforts will bear little fruit; our hearts must reach beyond the doing action. I believe that this is the mystery of the art pursued by the samurai, entertainers, and art lovers of that era. There is a beautifully written tanka poem that expresses this, "The moon does not think about its being reflected, and neither does the water in Lake Hirosawa think about its reflecting the moonshine." If one masters the state of detachment, one can make progress, regardless of the place and the art form.

Creating and Seeing

Mineshima: So far we have talked about your "production", but to us there is also the aspect of appreciation, that is, looking at a painting.

I think for you, production is the main area, but what are your views on "production" and "seeing", that is, creating and seeing? I believe there are views that creating and seeing are the same, but how do you feel about this?

Hamano: Well, I have been producing with the belief that seeing and creating are the same.

As artists, we are creating something, but ultimately, it doesn't matter if I don't create it; it will possibly be created by following generations. So if I stick too closely to production, I will undoubtedly lose sight of anything beyond that stage. I do not believe that "creating" is something that is exclusive to the artists, the giving side. I believe that among the art followers, the receiving side, there are many who are "creating". That is, even people who are not physically creating anything are creating something within their own lives. So if we consider that there are dais numbers of these admirable people, we can see that artists are not the only ones that create something. I am convinced that what is taught and learnt through discussions with people of thought not directly connected with art is especially important to those who will tackle art in the Future. And I believe that "object" creators will not be able to create a truly "good object" unless they completely absorb this point into their entire system.

If we think in this way, there are two ways of "seeing", one is simply through the eyes, while the other is through the heart. When I was fifteen, my mother asked a sculptor, Mr Hirao, to make an image of Buddha. After he finished, he brought it to my house. It was wrapped with many layers of white silk cloth and he carried it so tightly in both hands, just as if he were carrying a valuable treasure. I don't think my mother knew what was inside the white silk until she folded it back and actually saw the image. But she said she could see the image of Buddha inside the cloth as soon as she saw the person who created it.

The Worlds of Art Harmonise

The essential meaning of art, that is, "sow the seeds, plant the seedlings," indicates labour that is related to production, that is related to production, fundamental in an agricultural society. In ancient China, Greece and Rome, it was necessary and natural for all fully-fledged members of society to take up this study and skill, having been widely interpreted as being something fundamentally linked with life itself, as the skills for production and the means for surviving. This concept of art persisted in Japan until the eighteenth century, and gave rise to the unique Japanese culture handed down to us today. However, in modern society, our essential basic concept of art is being practically forgotten, overshadowed by the Japanese economy, and art is now barely surviving amidst a flood of controversy. We must not ignore the fact that misinterpreted forms of art are being made much of. As a consequence of the overipeness of capitalism, as well as the advance of social specialisation, the concept of modern art had brought forth many contradictions such as specialization even in the domain of personal values. In our present society, it is most important for artists to reconsider the essence of art and make inquiries from different angles. And what is most significant for the artist to grasp is the "shape or style" created in the past, and the "mental track" which he has been combating with great difficulty. The essence of twentieth century art can clearly be approached from the following three points of view. First of all, how a painting can break out of being fiction different from reality, able to approach reality and matter itself Secondly, paintings drawn on the flatness of a plane surface must give a sense of infinitely expanding space beyond the picture frame.

Thirdly, It is important to see how the artist's creative activity itself is being directly expressed in the form of a sense of life in the painting. This is inquiring into the roots of creation. The artist must polish and perfect his own creativity and originality, and also partake in an art movement as a group. I feel the artist's sense of being is that in which he battles against social mechanisms and commonly accepted thought and creates new and unknown values.

It is to carve the way to a new and unique world within a different dimension surpassing the bounds of East and West, firmly ground in Japanese tradition. On this occasion I exhibited a new work in trilogy form entitled *Sanjo* (pagoda) entrusting within it the concept which must be attained by artists in such a society of a new era.

Ichijo, called *Syomonjo*, means to hear widely and become enlightened. That is to say, one must try to hear even that which one's own ears cannot hear. *Nijo*", called *Enkakujo*, means to see and take note of everything. In other words, one must try to see even that which one's own eyes cannot see. When cherry blossom petals flutter in the winds, how far and intense do people try to penetrate with their eyes? In *Ichijo* and *Nijo* one strives to follow the very moment the petals fall to the ground, witness the reality of their fall, and catch the slightest sounds. In *Sanjo*, called *Bosatujo*, after becoming capable of *Ichijo* and *Nijo* one overcomes them and becomes firm and stable, becoming capable of judging things from a wider standpoint in a larger realm of thought. This is linked to achieving the pure and genuine new concept of art perhaps conceivable by inspiration in the next era.

On approaching the end of the twentieth century, we artists must not cease our inquiries into problems of creativity which might surface other words, one in the twenty-first century. And it is also important. that we lead the way towards a physical and spiritual world for our stream of consciousness of contempovary society.

(Extract from Sansai Art Magazine, Tokyo, March, 1989)

Toshihiro Hamano

Being between East and West

One of the difficulties in the world of art is the issue of nationalism or insularism. Natural "forms" and "quality" are deeply rooted in the culture and history of a nation . Nevertheless, my basic perception is that no art should be considered as belonging to and being confined to a certain country . It is true that when two different cultures of the West and the East encounter and compete with each other, we see their distinct diversities and qualities. However, we must pursue creativity that transcends such "provincialism".

Historical review of Japanese culture reveals two important hallmarks of Japanese art-emotion and patterns represented by the *Rinpa*, a school of painting initiated by Ogata Korin and the simple, outright and concentrated method of the *suiboku-ga* (black-and white drawing). These two make the essence of the "description of reality". Reality in Oriental art is characterised by unseparated time and space with *ma* (pause) linking the two. But only the superficial from of such tradition is retained today, leaving to oblivion the principle of "feeling things close to ourselves", and pitting tradition against the past, let alone the present. Another reason for the oblivion lies in the uncritical intake of Western nationalism since Japan opened its doors to the world outside. This uncriticality has caused the state of chaos as we see today.

Exchanges in the area of art should not bring both sides down to equal levels. Instead they should help them *pursue in-depth probe* of their own problems on an equal footing. This is the world's realistic theme of connecting East and West cultures on a new level. I believe that artists engaged in such activities must be those who create values unknown to the world. With this unlimited imagination and originality, they should be able to join hands for the development of art and have good understanding of the social structure and the future outlook. Cultural exchanges become realistic only when they

Fig.6   Hamano was invited as committee of International
        Triennial of Drawing,Kunsthalle Nürnberg, 1988

cooperate in crossing national borders and
overcoming cultural barriers.

contemporary art group *Ryu* was
established in 1971 and has endeared to
bring the world of contemporary art closer to
people. *Ryu* is not only a group of artists but is
the core of activities for reforming the
environment and constructing a new order.
Since 1984, the group has conducted
international exchanges in the art world by
holding the Contemporary Art Exhibition in
Yugoslavia and Austria, inviting many artists
and art organizations to Japan, organizing art
exhibitions, and dispatching art students
overseas. These activities are prompted by a
belief that art is based on the actions and spirit
of man who is engaged in ceaseless artistic
pursuit.

(Extract from **IV** International Triennial of Drawing,
Nürnberg, exh. cat.,1988)

Toshihiro Hamano

The Spirit of the *Ryu* Group

"The moon does not think about its being
reflected, and neither does the water in Lake
Hirosawa think about its reflecting the
moonshine." (A well-known saying of a Zen
master.)

We know a lot about Japan, its exciting
history and culture, its people and their life,
and especially about its fast economic
development after World War **II** .
We can no longer imagine being without
Japanese electronic products.

The situation in art, especially in "Japanese
art of today", is reversed. The information
input is very low, if there is any at all. This is
why it seems so important to fill in the gaps
with new knowledge.
gradually decrease, and at

The self-centred European thought is still
limited. This prevailing one-sidedness will the
same time new perspectives will open up.
This is the reason why we find it so important
to show the *Ryu* group (established in 1971 in
Japan), after its exhibition in Austria and
Yugoslavia, here in Germany for the first time,
at the Kunsthalle in Dürer's town Nüremberg.

The creativity of the artists of the group is
very diverse. Along with painting and
sculpture, we also find many experimental
works. Moreover, there are some artists in the
Ryu group who are seriously engaged in
redesigning the environment for the needs of a
new society. The group is a reservoir of
artistic activities without any stylistic
limitation. The group spirit, the feeling of
belonging to one another generates strength
and creative power. Through this, it is possible
to include younger artists and help them to
find, through the experience of the older ones,
their own way while the ultimate aim remains
open.

The spirit of the *Ryu* group is full of great
vivacity and diversity. Its champion is Toshihiro
Hamano, who was very important in figure to
the forming of the group with his personal artistic
work as well as with his mental attitude. He
also acts as a father of the *Ryu* group help

Fig.7   Hamano performing in Kunsthalle Nürnberg, 1988

to solve the problems occuring within the group, and leads it towards success. For the distinguished artist who has won many important prizes, this represents, along with his own creativity, a life task he has set to himself.

(Extract from Hamano and Ryu, exh. cat., Nürnberg, 1988)

Curt Heigl
Director of The Kunsthalle Nürnberg

The Art of Toshihiro Hamano
—Between Wind and Storm—

The basis for Toshihiro Hamano's art, as it is perceived by a Western mind at least, is like the friction between wind and storm. It is like difference between potential energy-suggestions of which are caught in the paintings-and the violence found when switching from potential to kinetic energy. It addresses the great dilemma: whether to limit-and thus control-the potential in a painting, or whether to set this energy free, and allow an external flowing spiral of the two forces.

Again and again, we are excited and filled with admiration for this genre of art-the best example of which is Hamano. This excitement flows from two things. Firstly, because through Hamano's strict simplification, his art has not only reached the value of symbolism, but it has also managed to merge an architecturally sculptured approach with the most refined rules of design. Secondly, he excites through the violence of the geometric shapes, in his paintings.

These are as powerful as those in "action paintings", but in Hamano's work, this is reversed to give a very precise and accurate performance at the same time.

At a first glance, the artist's imaginative powers seem inexhausible: the varieties and combinations of the interlacings in his line-based creations; filling the space and mastering the painting's surface with the flair of a calligrapher and the consistancy of an architect; he displays rationality as well as visionariness, and addresses directly the question of what to paint creatively means at the advent of the twenty-first century-or at least as far as this is understood by us looking at the problem from the end of this century.

Some dramatic effects, such as the rare use of colour, give an almost surrealist dimension to his work, appearing to intervene in the cosmic spaciousness of his canvases. The carelessness which is conjured up in Hamano's painting by a contlolled or free sling, varies between being of an almost physical nature, materialised in the black space, and being of a spiritual nature symbolising the bouyancy of the human spirit which cannot be repressed.

When an observer's eye follows the lights and the shades of the rolling steel and the shrill breaking of black stone, his or her imagination is following the dynamic and the static-in other words, the two essential forces of our understanding and control of the human world. Flashes of enlightenment come from above, and the observer is fread from the limiting boundaries in which our minds are tied down.

Hamano's line, a product of the intellect, is a masterly experiment which illustrates the conditionality of our existence-something which cannot easily be expressed in words.

Fig.8   Zoran Kržišnik in Moderna galerija, ljubljana, 1985

We strive to understand the meaning of existence, to capture it and to adjust it to our needs and desires, hoping to change what is frightening and unknowable into permanent, eternal gifts. At the same time, however, we are aware that we are reaching for the impossible, yet attempting this is the only thing which gives our life any sense or direction.

The elegance of Hamano's symbolism, simultaneously flowing and full of motion, as well as being forbiddingly static like the hard shell hiding the action taking place within it, this elegance leads us into the future, into the merging of the spiritual and material forces of the East and the West, which is expected to happen in assume that the control of everything (at the moment achieved only through purely plastic art) will also be possible through design.

(Extract from Toshihiro Hamano, exh. cat., Galerie de Francony, Tokyo, 1988)

Zoran Kržišnik
Director International Centre of Graphic Arts in Ljubljana

Hamano and Ljubljana

Once again, the Ljubljana Modern Gallery has the special pleasure of staging an exhibition of the *Ryu* group. This year the exhibition will also include an one-man show of the leader of the group, Toshihiro Hamano. Exhibitions this group have always been notable events for the Ljubljana public. At first, the public reacted more out of interest in a remote and alien culture; later on it was, however, more and more the artistic quality of the exhibited works that attracted their attention. Our public are now already acquainted with the group, which is to a great extent thanks to some of the younger members who come for post-graduate studies to Ljubljana, where as a rule they quickly become part of its artistic and cultural life. This time we are particularly pleased that the exhibition in preparation will now, after so

many years of successful cooperation with our Japanese friends, be shown not only in Ljubljana, but also in two important German artistic centres.

International Biennial of Graphic Art in Ljubljana has proved to be for many Japanese artist a point of departure toward recognition and merited acclaim outside their own country. Thanks to the exhibitions of the *Ryu* group, our public have recently got the opportunity to come to know and respect not only graphic achievements, but also contemporary Japanese painting and sculpture. As far as we can afford to make generalizations in writing about art, we can State that with good Japanese artists, and this country always takes care to represent itself through the best, we admire the synthesis achieved by combining their technical and working discipline, with liberalism and with a traditionally and historically disparate imagination and conception of what a work of art should be. The sensibility of Japanese artists is usually rudimentary, stinted in its means of expression, but this is precisely why it is so much more eloquent. It is a contemplative silence that not only narrates, but speaks, sometimes whispering, and sometimes screaming. We are repeatedly fascinated by the Japanese artists' attitude towards the process of creation. They have a professional attitude towards the very last detail, -sometimes to such a degree that, by Western criteria, we ask ourselves whether this perfection does not perhaps even affect the expressiveness of their work. These, however, are details which, of a Western man formed by his own tradition of civilisation demand discernment, comprehension and empathy with the past and present of the cultural and social history of the East.

The strict selection of the artists of the *Ryu* group has, through its sensitive forms, volumes and colours, always known how to relate to the Slovene public. To the viewer who loves art to the extent that he tries to approach it totally unburdened and relaxed, who can with all his being immerse himself in the depth of its essence, the work of the

Japanese artists has always communicated the profound message of its civilization.

(Extract from Hamano and *Ryu*, exh. cat., Ljubljana, 1989)

Jure Mikuž
Director of The Ljubljana Modern Gallery

Comments

It is said that the ancient province of Sanuki (present-day Kagawa Prefectura) had the largest number of Shinto shrines and Buddhist temples per capita. And it is amidst this area of scenic tranquillity that the artist Toshihiro Hamano has made his home, and has quietly sought to perfect his own artistic style.

When I cast my eyes across the huge Mandala flower painted by Toshihiro Hamano on the ceiling of Sakaide Kannonji temple I could not but marvel at the talent of this artist. The brightness of the painting seems to radiate great warmth. While showing the influence of Buddhism and its tradition spanning many centuries, the painting has a refreshing and joyful air that is highly in keeping with the hearts of the Japanese people. As we draw close to the end of the twentieth century, this work will undoubtedly be admired by many people as argurably the best Mandala painting executed this century.

I was amazed at the way he became completely engrossed as he leaned over a large canvas working on his latest *sumie* painting. The air was filled with the seriousness of a sword-fight to the death in old Japan.

I cannot comprehend abstract art, but Toshihiro Hamano's work is without sarcasm and rich in thought. The trilogy entitled "San-jo" (Three Ways), exhibited as a background to my public lecture at the hall in the Academy of Comparative Philosophy at the end of last October, is said to express the three Buddhist ideals of Bodhisattva-yana (the way of the pre-enlightened Buddha), Pratyeka-buddha-yana(the way of the self-enlightened Buddha) and Sravaka-yana (the way of the disciple), and it does so splendidly. I believe that his work, which was passionately inspired by the Byodoin temple in Uji, expresses with great realism the ideals and longings of its creators in the Heian period (late eighth — early twelfth century).

Toshihiro Hamano's work is rich in thought because as well as being an artist, he is a free-thinking philosopher. He describes his theories of art in his recently published book *Geijutsu no Iso wo Kataru* (About the Phases of Art), and his strength and ability to vivify tradition will see him soar to great heights. His headquarters have been established in the 21st Century International Exchange Art Academy in Sakaide City, and I am deeply moved by the enthusiasm of his many followers.

Hajime NaKamura
Philosopher

I have known Toshihiro Hamano for many years, and I always see him whenever he holds an exhibition in Tokyo. However, this is not as often as I should like, for he has made his home so. far away.

I consider myself to be well-versed in his work. We must not overlook the fact that, unlike the works of many other painters, his abstract work has an originality uninfluenced by foreign styles. He presents new forms one after another with great force, and with perfect harmony between his mind, spirit and hands, Toshihiro Hamano will continue to give life to a wide range of artistic ideas. His book *Geijutsu no Iso wo Kataru*s, I believe, one such creation.

Ichiro Fukuzawa
Painter

Toshihiro Hamano is endowed with a natural gift shared by very few. With roots firmly established in Shikoku, he continues to produce works of art rich in individuality.

His work does not echo that of others; every piece is full of the rays of originality. When I saw his work in Nürnberg and Köln, I could feel that it was influenced by neither the West nor the East. If I must say, his work has an air of universality.

In art a sense of being at one with regional life is important. When asked the reason for his living in such a provincial area as Vienna, Brahms responded, "I am the kind of person who can live only in the country." And the work of Brahms has now become the spiritual food of people throughout the world.

Be it through paintings or the written word, what Toshihiro Hamano seeks to portray is his philosophy and universal truth.

Yoichiro Omachi
Musician

Fig.9   Central part of Mandala, by Hamano

Fig.10 Ceiling Painting Mandala, Sakaide Kannon-ji

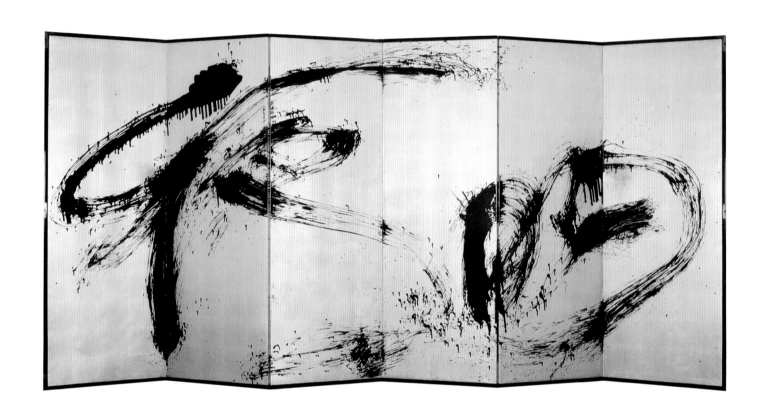

Fig.11 "YOAKE (Dawn)"
   Darkness which has remained closed is brightly opened up by a streak of light.

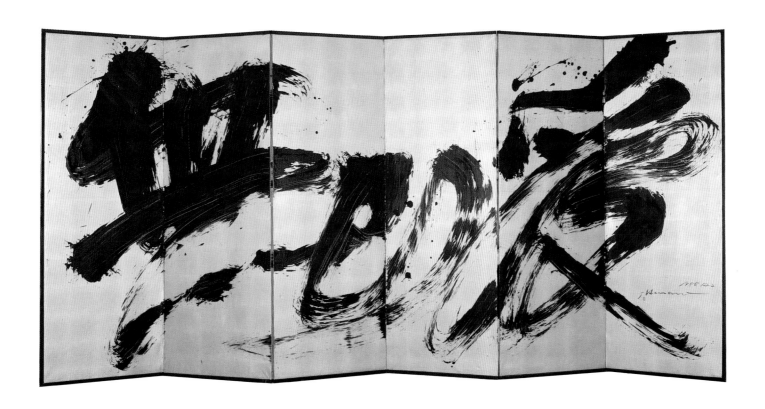

Fig.12 "MU-SOKU-AI (Assimilation of Nothingness and Agapae)"
Nothingness (or emptiness) which symbolizes the Orient instantaneously assimilates with agapae (or mercy) which represents the Occident.

Fig.13 "DEAI (Through communication of love)"
An encounter is broughl forth by communicating the power of "love".

Toshihiro Hamano Biography

Toshihiro Hamano was born in Osaka on 6 December 1937.
His father, Tatsuji, was a dyer, and his mother, Tane, was a devout and religious woman.
At the end of the Second World War, the family moved to Takamatsu, a city famous for the many Buddhist temples there.

1957   Enters the Tama University of Fine Art, Western painting course, Tokyo   Reads the books written by Taisetz Suzuki, Zen master
1961   Graduates from the University and moves to Takamatsu
1966   Begins to work the paintings based on Mandala's thought
1968   Begins to sit in meditation in Zen Temple, Zuiouji, Ehime
1971   Establishes the Ryu Contemporary Art Group   First trip to the West Germany, Holland, France and Italy
1972   Hamano devoted himself to the creation of the series of monumental works of Mandala in an effort to discern the limit of the body and the spirit of a human being. He was to further pursue for another ten years the unique art of his own, the expression of metal strips which had been worked out from the series.
1974   Meets the comparative philosopher Hideo Mineshima
1975   "The World of Toshihiro Hamano" is produced by Seiichiro Suzuki, NHK broad cast
1977   Becomes a member of the Academy of Comparative Philosophy
1978   Creates his first outdoor environmental sculpture, "Tower of Love"
Since then, he has continued to create public works: sculptures, gardens, murals, ceiling paintings, etc.
1979   Establishes Gallery Tableau 5 in Sakaide in order to introduce the world of contemporary art and promote the young artists
1980   "The Experiment of Toshihiro Hamano" is produced by Yoshiki Nishimura, NHK broad cast
1981   Initiates the creation of works of trigonal prisms. The architectonic expression of black and white is an attempt to visualise Oriental and Occidental philosophy.
1982   Receives "Art and Culture Award" for his meritorious works from Tatsuo Banjo, Mayor of Sakaide City.
1985   Receives "Shikoku Shinbun Culture Award".
1985   Founds Gallery Tableau, ∞ Mugen. Visits Ljubljana, in Yugoslavia to hold an exhibition Meets Zoran Kržišnik, Director of the Moderna garelerija Ljubljana and Andrej Jemec, Painter
1988   Curt Heigl, Director of Kunsthalle Nürnberg and Wolfgang Horn, the curator visit Hamano Takamatsu and Sakaide
Invited by Nürnberg Triennial organizers as a member of the committee Travels to Nürnberg, Köln, and Berlin to hold solo exhibition and he meets Yoichiro Omachi, the conductor and his son Raifu, a musician who together wrote some music influenced by Hamano's performance
1989   Organizes the lecture on conparative philosophy in Sakaide
Meets Hajime Nakamura, philosopher Writtes, "About the Phase of Art; conversation with Hideo Mineshima" conversation by Hokuju Publishing Co. Mugen in Takamatsu
1990   Designed a *Karesansui* (dry landscaped) Japanese garden in Sanuki Sanjoso, a Kyoto cuisine restaurant in Kagawa-cho.

Lives and works in takamatsu, Japan

One-Person Exhibitions

1971 Wallraf — Richartz Art Museum, Köln
1972 Kunugi Gallery,Tokyo, "Toshihiro Hamano: Mandala"(exh. cat., text by Taro Nomura)
1974 Kunugi Gallery, Tokyo
1975 Shibuya Contemporary Art Center, Tokyo
     Kunugi Gallery,Tokyo
1976 Kunugi Gallery,Tokyo
1977 Kagawa Prefectural Culture Hall, Takamatsu,"Toshihiro Hamano: Paintings, Installation"(exh. cat.)
1978 Okabe Gallery, Tokyo
1979 Kunugi Gallery, Tokyo
1980 Ginza Mikimoto Gallery, Tokyo, "Toshihiro Hamano: JuJu-Mujin"(exh. cat., text by Ichiro Hariu)
1983 Ginza Emba Cultural Hall, Tokyo,"Toshihiro Hamano: His life time of this decade"(exh. cat., text by Ichiro Hariu)
1984 Moderna galerija, Ljubljana,"The World of Toshihiro Hamano"(exh. cat.)
1985 Moderna galerija, Ljubljana,"Toshihiro Hamano and His Pupils"(exh. cat., text by Zoran Kržišnik)
     Kärntner Landesgalerie, Klagenfurt, Austria,"Toshihiro Hamano and His pupils"(exh. cat., text by Karl Newole)
     Palais palffy, Wien,"Toshihiro Hamano"(exh. cat., text by Herbert Moritz)
1986 Kagawa Prefectural Culture Hall, Takamatsu,"Toshihiro Hamano: Retrospective Exhibition"
1987 Sakaide Art Museum, Sakaide,"Toshihiro Hamano and Artists of Ryu"(exh. cat.)
1988 Galerie de Francony, Tokyo,"Toshihiro Hamano: Paintings, Prints"(exh. cat., text by Zoran Kržišnik)
     Taishodo Gallery, Fujisawa,"Toshihiro Hamano: Paintings, Prints"
     Nürnberger Kunsthalle, Nürnberg,"Hamano and Ryu"(exh. cat., text by Curt Heigl)

1989 Japanisches Kulturinstitut, Köln,"Hamano and Ryu"(exh. cat., text by Yoichiro Omachi)
     Moderna galerija, Ljubljana,"Hamano and Ryu"(exh. cat., text by Jure Mikuž)
     Space Sakaide, Sakaide,"Toshihiro Hamano: Drawing in India ink"
1990 Space Sakaide, Sakaide,"Toshihiro Hamano: Paintings, Prints"
1991 Space Sakaide, Sakaide,"Drawings of Toshihiro Hamano"

Selected Group Exhibitions

1968 Takamatsu City Museum,"Shikoku Contemporary Art Exhibition" (Hamano was awarded the secound prize)
     Kagawa prefectural Culture Hall, Takamatsu, "Kagawa Contemporary Art Exhibition" (Hamano was awarded the first prize)
1974 Tokyo Central Museum, Tokyo, "The 9th Japan Art Festival"(also traveled in Canada to Musee d' Art Contemporain, Montreal; Vancouver Art Gallery, Vancouver)
1975 Tokyo Metropolitan Museum, Tokyo, "The 10th Japan Art Festival" (also traveled in New Zealand and Australia to National Art Gallery, Wellington; National Queensland Art Museum, Queensland)
     Tokyo Metropolitan Museum, Tokyo, "The 11th Contemporary Art Exhibition of Japan" (Hamano was awarded the second prize)
     Gallery Will, Paris, "40 Japanese Contemporary Artists"
     Tokyo Metropolitan Museum, Tokyo, "The 1st Tokyo Exhibition -'75 Art Highlight- Development of Abstract"

1976 Tokyo Metropolitan Museum, Tokyo, "The 12th Contemporary Art Exhibition of Japan" (also traveled to National Museum of Modern Art Kyoto, Kyoto) Tokyo Metropolitan Museum, Tokyo, "The 11th Japan Art Festival" (also traveled to The Art Museum, Washington and Los Angeles)

1977 Tokyo Metropolitan Museum, Tokyo, "The 13th Contemporary Art Exhibition of Japan" (also traveled to National Museum of Modern Art Kyoto, Kyoto) Kagawa Prefectural Culture Hall, "The 1st 10 Contemporary Artists in Kagawa"

1978 Emba Art Museum, Ashiya, "The 1st Japan Emba Annual"

1979 Tokyo Metropolitan Museum, Tokyo, "The 14th Contemporary Art Exhibition of Japan" (Hamano was awarded the prize of Gunma Prefectural Modern Art Museum)(also traveled to National Museum of Modern Art Kyoto, Kyoto)

1980 Emba Art Museum, Ashiya, "The 3rd Japan Emba Annual" (Hamano was awarded the second prize)

1981 Emba Art Museum, Ashiya, "The 4th Japan Emba Annual"

1982 Emba Art Museum, Ashiya, "The 5th Japan Emba Annual" (Hamano was awarded the Grand-Prix)

1984 Paris, "Japan in Asia" Moderna galerija, Ljubljana, "Ryu-razstava"

1985 Kagawa Prefectural Culture Hall, Takamatsu "Ryu International Exhibition", organized in cooparation with the Bundesminister für Unterrict, Kunst und Sport, Wien, Embassy of Japan, Wien(also traveled to Moderna galerija, Ljubljana;Kärntner Landesgalerie, Klagenfurt;Palais Palffy, Wien) Moderna galerija, Ljubljana, "The 16th International Biennial of Graphic Art" New Delhi National Modern Art Museum, New Delhi, "The Message — Japanese Contemporary Art " (also

traveled to Sogo Art Museum, Yokohama, Japan, 1986)

1987 Moderna galerija, Ljubljana, "The 17th International Biennial of Graphic Art" Sakaide Art Museum, "Toshihiro Hamano and Artists of Ryu" organized in association with the Kagawa Art Festival, Kagawa Prefectural Board of Education.

1988 Sakaide Art Museum, Sakaide, "The International Biennial of Graphic Art, Ljubljana in Japan" organized in collaboration with International Centre of Graphic Arts, Ljubljana, and in association with the Ryu Contemporary Art (also traveled to Kawasaki City Museum, Kawasaki) Kunsthalle Nürnberg, "The 4th International Triennial of Drawing" (Hamano was invited as committee) Kunsthalle Nürnberg, "Hamano und Ryu", organized in cooparation with Kunsthalle Nürnberg, The Japan Foundation, Embassy of Japan, Bonn, Japanishes Kulturinstitut, Köln, (also traveled to Japanishes Kurturistitut, Köln, 1989 Moderna galerija, Ljubljana, 1989)

1989 "5th International Print Biennale", Varna, Burgaria

1991 Talbot Rice Gallery, Edinburgh "Zen: Hamano & Ryu", organized by The Japan Festival 1991 (also travel to Nothern Centre for Contemporary Art, Sunderland;Sala de Exposiciores de la Comunidad de Madrid, Spain)

Public Works

1978   Created his first outdoor environmetal sculpture, "Tower of Love", by stone (35t) for the courtyard of Sakaide City Hall, Sakaide
Worked on a wall painting, "Fly Away" for the Sakaide town hall, Sakaide

1979   Worked on a dry landscape garden,"Cho-Kan-Tei", (1800 m²) for the courtyard of Sakaide Ohashi Memorial Library, Sakaide

1981   Worked on a wall painting, "The Wing of Phenomenon" (2.5 X 1.5m) for the New Utazu town hall, Utazu
Woked on a wall painting, "Ohiri (full-house)" (88 X 200cm) for the Utazu Comunity Centre, Utazu

1982   Worked on a ceiling painting,"Mandala" (5.6 X 4.6m) for the Sakaide Kannonji temple, Sakaide

1983   Worked on a wall painting, "Eternity" (2.1 X 6.2m) for the gymnasium of Sakaide   Started the planning, "21st century Ars Island Project" for Koyoshima island on the Seto Inland Sea

1984   Worked on a wall painting, "Salt Farm" for the City library, Sakaide

1986   Worked on a ceiling painting, "Rising Dragon" (2.5 X 2.5m) for the Sakaide Kannonji temple, Sakaide

1987   Worked on a wall painting,"Work85-5" Kagawa Prefectural high school, Sakaide

1988   Worked on a drop curtain dyeing, "Seto Ohasi" (1.2 X 11.7m) for Sakaide Comunity Center, Sakaide

1989   Worked on a wall painting,"Work81-10" for the Pacific Hotel Nagisa, Sakaide

1990   Worked on a dry landscape garden, "Sanuki Sanjo-so", Kagawa

1991   Worked on a pillar sculpture,"Sea gull" for the Ryo-kei bridge, Sakaide
Worked on a pillar sculpture, "Hotaru" for the Hotaru-mi bridge, Manno,Kagawa

Public Collections

Kagawa Prefectural Culture Hall, Takamatsu, Japan
Sakaide Art Museum, Sakaide, Japan
Utazu City Hall, Utazu, Japan
Museum of Modern Art, Gunma, Japan
Museum of Modern Art, Saitama, Japan
Tochigi Prefectural Museum of Fine Arts, Tochigi, Japan
Moderna galerija, Ljubljana, Yugoslavia
Kärntner Landesgalerie Klagenfurt, Austria
Bundesminister für Unterrich, Kunst und Sport, Wien, Austria
Kunsthalle Nürnberg, Germany
Japanisches Kurturinstitut, Köln, Germany
The Embassy of Japan, Bonn, Germany
The Embassy of Japan, Madrid, Spain

Selected Bibliography

Louise Letocha, 'Contemporary Art from Japan.' Ateliers-Musee D'Art contemporain, Montreal, September 8, 1974

'Hamano and his pupils.' Sankei, Osaka. December 1, 1974

Yoshiaki Inui, 'Do away with the limitation of the painting.' Mainichi, Tokyo, June 11, 1975

Sadao Kato, 'Hamano was awarded the prize of the 14th Contemporary Art Exhibition of Japan.' Mainichi, Tokyo, April 21, 1979

Toshihiro Hamano, 'Where the abstract painting in Japan is.' Art Vision, Tokyo, September, 1979

'Hamano and Sakaide -his trial-.' Shikoku, Takamatsu, August 16, 1981

Sohei Fujimoto, 'Toshihiro Hamano, Work79-10' Art Top, Tokyo, February, 1982

'Hamano, Work82-1' Yomiuri, Tokyo, October 26, 1982

'Toshihiro Hamano, Grand-Prix at Emba.' Shikoku, Takamatsu, November 28, 1982

Koujin Tanaka, 'Review, Hamano's personal exhibition in Tokyo. 'Mainichi, Tokyo, June 1, 1983

Tsuyoshi Kanazawa, 'Toshihiro Hamano: Modern Beat.' Art Top, Tokyo, no.73, February, 1983

'Interview with Toshihiro Hamano -light and shadow-.' The Shinbijutsu Shinbun, Tokyo, July 11, 1983

Taro Nomura, 'Interview with Toshihiro Hamano.' Art Vision, Tokyo, August, 1983

Tenmei Fujisawa, 'Toshihiro Hamano's New Works.' Art Graph, Tokyo, vol.4, no.7, August, 1983

'Japanese Group Exhibition in Ljubljana Modern Gallery Toshihiro Hamano: traditional spirit.' Dnevnik, Ljubljana, June 6, 1984

Marijan Zlobec, 'From Small Japanese Town to The World-through Ljubljana.' Delo, Ljubljana, June 8, 1984

'Hamano in Yugoslavia.' The Shinbijutsu Shinbun, Tokyo, July 1, 1984

Janez Mesesnel, 'Group Ryu from Japan.' Delo, Ljubljana, July 4, 1984

'Pick Up; Toshihiro Hamano in Ljubljana.' Art Top, Tokyo, no.82, August, 1984

'Art Group Ryu: International Cultural Exchange.' Zephyros, Okayama, no.2, December, 1984

'Toshihiro Hamano: The 25th Shikoku Culture Prize.' Shikoku, Takamatsu, January 22, 1985

'Ryu' Art Top, Tokyo, no.86, April, 1985

Janez Mesesnel, 'Japanese Art, Group Ryu in Modern Gallery.' Delo, Ljubljana, April 10, 1985

Franz Zalar, 'Group Ryu in Ljubljana Modern Gallery, Art World of Japan.' Dnevnik, Ljubljana, April 13, 1985

Michael Kuscher, 'Group Ryu in Landesgalerie Klagenfurt.' KTZ, Klagenfurt, May 24, 1985

Lei, 'Ryu from Japan.' Kleine Zeitung, Klagenfurt, May 25, 1985

Ilse Bromme, 'Japanese Ryu Group in Landesgalerie.' NVZ, Klagenfurt, May 31, 1985

Uhl, 'Japanese Art.' Kärntner Landeszeitung, Klagenfurt, May 30, 1985

H.G.Pribil, 'Contemporary Art from Japan, Exhibition of Ryu Group in Palais Palffy.' Wiener Zeitung, Wien, July 24, 1985

'Hamano, Homage to The Great Sun.' Shikoku, Takamatsu, October 5, 1985

'Dialogue between Hamano and Taro Okamoto.' Shikoku, Takamatsu, November 18, 1985

'The Message.' Mainichi, Tokyo, February 3, 1986

'Sakaide Art Museum and local community.' Shikoku, Takamatsu, March 11, 1986

'Hamano, his experience for 15years in Sakaide.' The Shinbijutsu Shinbun, Tokyo, June 1, 1986

Breda Protnar, '10 Japanese Artists.' Dnevnik, Ljubljana, December 11, 1986

Joze Pojbic, 'Japanese Artists.' Delo, Ljubljana, December 18, 1986

Nace Bizilj, 'Japanese Exhibition at Komiteju za Kulturo.' Dnevnik, Ljubljana, December 18, 1986

Marijan Tršar, 'Japanese Perfection.' Razgledi po svetu, Ljubljana, January 30, 1987

Kimihiko Matsuura, 'Toshihiro Hamano and

Ryu, his activities and public works.' Asahi,
Tokyo, April 21, 1987
'Toshihiro Hamano, Over the Limit.' Shiloku,
Takamatsu, September 27, 1987
'Toshihiro Hamano, The Bridge from Sakaide
to The World.' The Shinbijutsu Shinbun,
Tokyo, February, 1988
'Toshihiro Hamano: Ljubljana and Japan.'
Sansai, Tokyo, no.491, August, 1988
'Hamano: Triangle and Belt, East and West.'
Mainichi, Tokyo, September 15, 1988
'Toshihiro Hamano, A Day of Artist.' Art
Vision, Tokyo, vol.16, no.2, September, 1988
'Hamano, International Triennial of Drawing,
Nürnberg.' Sankei, Tokyo, no.492, September,
1988
'Hamano and Ryu: Art Now.' Ehime,
Matsuyama, October 17, 1988
'Hamano and Space Sakaide.' Shikoku,
Takamatsu, November 2, 1988
Walter Fenn, 'Toshihiro Hamano, The Petrified
Wind.' Nürnberger Nachrichten, Nürnberg,
December 3, 1988
Klaus Martin Wiese, 'Art Worlds are Fusing.'
Abend Zeitung, Nürnberg, December 3, 1988
Halef, 'Hamano, Solidification of the wind.'
Nürnberger Zeitung, December 3, 1988
'Hamano in Germany: Sanjo.' Sankei, Tokyo,
December 4, 1988
F.J.Broder,'Hamano and Ryu in Nürnberg.'
Frankischer Tag, Bamberg, December 7, 1988
'Hamano and Ryu in Germany.' Mainichi,
Tokyo, December 10, 1988
'From local to the world.' The Shinbijutsu
Shinbun, Tokyo, December 11, 1988
'Toshihiro Hamano -Performance-.' Asiya
Osaka, December 13, 1988
'Toshihiro Hamano: Letter from Europe.'
Sansai, Tokyo, no.498, March, 1989
'Dialogue between Hamano and Taro
Okamoto.' Shikoku, Takamatsu, September 19,
1990
'Interview to Toshihiro Hamano and Duncan
Macmillan.' Shikoku, Takamatsu, June 19, 1991

Tsuishu-Gohshi (Lacquer ware, incense container) by Seiji Ohata, 1990

Incense was introduced from India along with Buddhism, and has been handed down in the tea ceremony besides in the religion. The purpose is to purify one's body and mind with incense, and it is commonly offered in an incense container placed in an alcove of houses.

Mr. Ohata who originated this technique which takes a long time (it takes at least three years to complete one work) taught Hamano when he was a high school student, and since then Hamano has been on very precious terms with his teacher.

List of works
Toshihiro Hamano

1. Homage to the Great Sun 1965
   oil and acrylic on canvas
   162.0×130.3cm

2. Variational aspects of *Mandala*-4 1972
   oil and acrylic on canvas
   194.0×130.3cm

3. Work73-5 1973
   oil and acrylic on canvas
   130.0×194.0cm

4. Work75-2 Crease 1975
   oil and acrylic on acrylboard
   119.0×162.0×0.5cm

5. Work75-4 1975
   oil and acrylic on acrylboard
   83.0×151.5×0.5cm
   coll.,Kagawa Prefectural Culture Hall

6. Work75-5 Beginning 1975
   acrylic on wooden board
   123.0×160.0×2.5cm

7. Work76-1 1976
   oil and acrylic on granite
   (160.0×23.0×2.3)cm×5

8. Work77-3 1977
   oil and acrylic on wooden board
   88.0×200.0×2.5cm

9. Work79-2 1979
   oil and acrylic on silk
   240.0×150.0cm

10. Work79-7 1979
    oil and acrylic on canvas
    162.0×390.9cm

11. Work79-10 Jiu Jiu mujin-(abow tie) 1979
    oil and acrylic on canvas
    181.8×227.3cm

12. Work80-6 Jiu Jiu mujin-(abow tie)1980
    oil and acrylic on acrylboard
    118.0×100.0×66.0cm

13. Work82-1 1982
    oil and acrylic on stainless steel
    130.3×162.0cm

14. Work83-4 Azekura 1983
    oil and acrylic on canvas
    193.9×130.3cm

15. Work84-5 The God of Wind 1984
    oil and acrylic gold foil on fold screen
    161.0×181.8cm

16. Work84-5 The God of Thunder 1984
    oil and acrylic gold foil on fold screen
    161.0×181.8cm

17. Work86-1 kukai 1986
    oil and acrylic on fold screen
    184.0×232.0cm

18. Work88-1 Shomonjo(Pagoda) 1988
    oil and acrylic on canvas
    227.3×130.3cm

19. Work88-2 Enkakujo(Pagoda) 1988
    oil and acrylic on canvas
    227.3×130.3cm

20. Work88-3 Bosatsujo(Pagoda) 1988
    oil and acrylic on canvas
    227.3×130.3cm

21. Work88-1 Shomonjo(Pagoda)
    Lithography
    90.0×51.6cm

22. Transparency projected on the paintings
    Work88-2 Enkakujo(Pagoda)

23. Transparency projected on the paintings
    Work88-3 Bosatsujo(Pagoda)

24. Work88-5 Atelier 1988
    oil and acrylic on canvas
    362.2×227.3cm

25. Work88-4 Tendan 1988
    oil and acrylic on canvas
    227.3×181.3cm

26. Setting in Banshoen garden
    Work88-6 Pagoda 1988

27. Work88-6 Pagoda 1988
    oil and acrylic on canvas
    181.8×454.6cm

28. Work91-1 Teahouse 1991
    oil and acrylic on canvas
    227.3×145.5cm

29. Work91-2 Tokonoma and
    Nijiriguchi 1991
    oil and acrylic on canvas
    227.3×291.0cm

30. Work91-3 Opened Gate 1991
    oil and acrylic on canvas
    227.3×130.3cm

31. Working Sketch for Work82-1

32. Working Sketch for Series of Pagoda

33. Working Sketch for Series of Pagoda

34. Sketch for Work88-3 Bosatsujo(Pagoda)

Catalogue of Works by Toshihiro Hamano

Cat.1

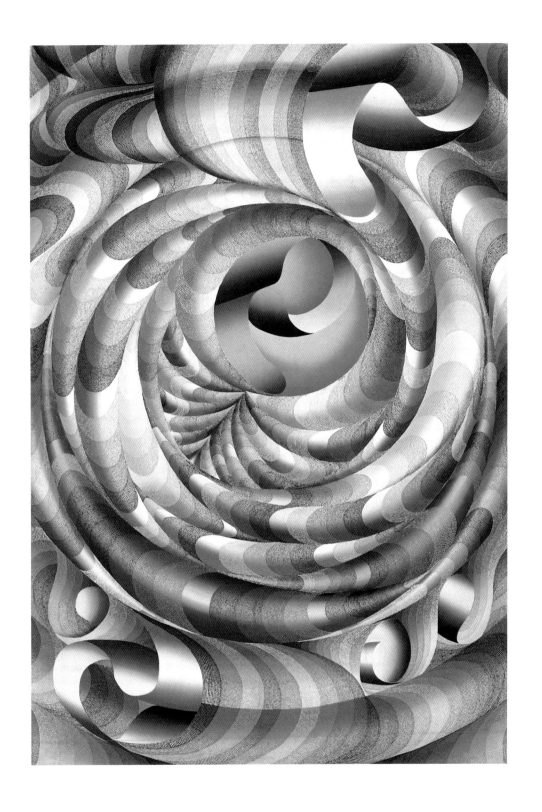

Cat.2

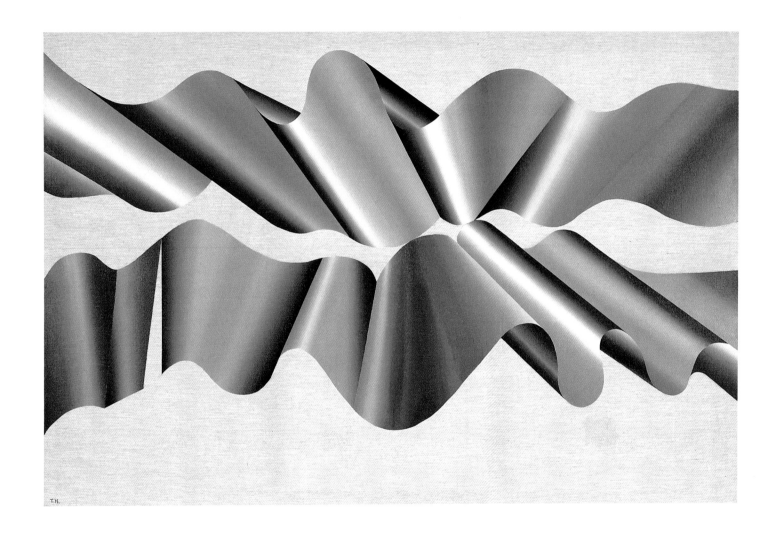

Cat.3

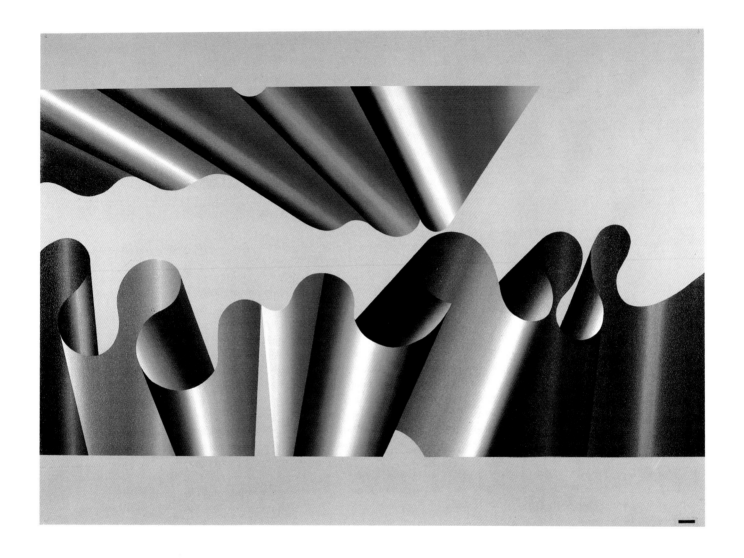

Cat. 4

Cat.5

Cat.6

Cat.7

Cat.8

Cat.9

Cat.10

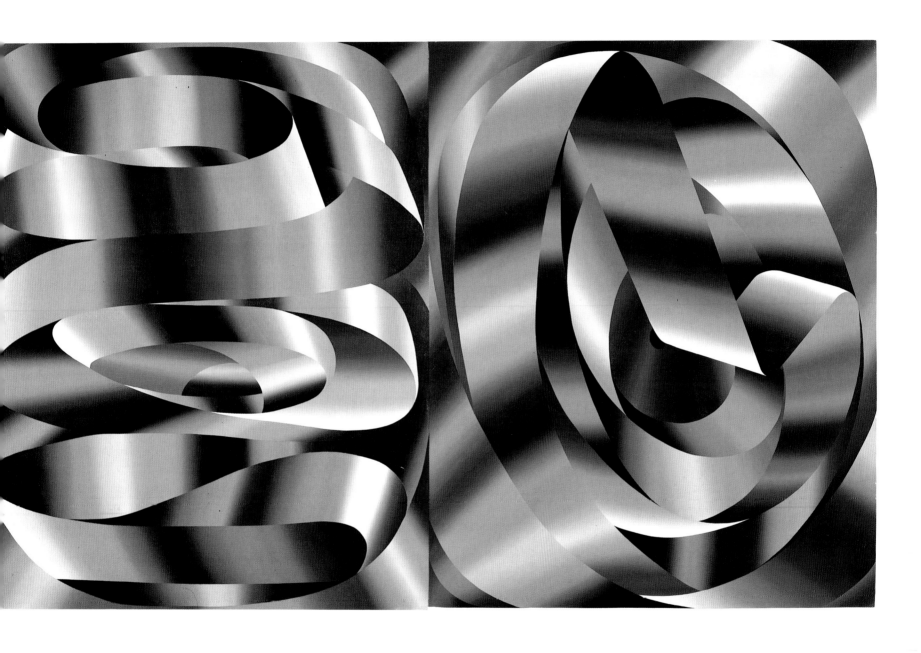

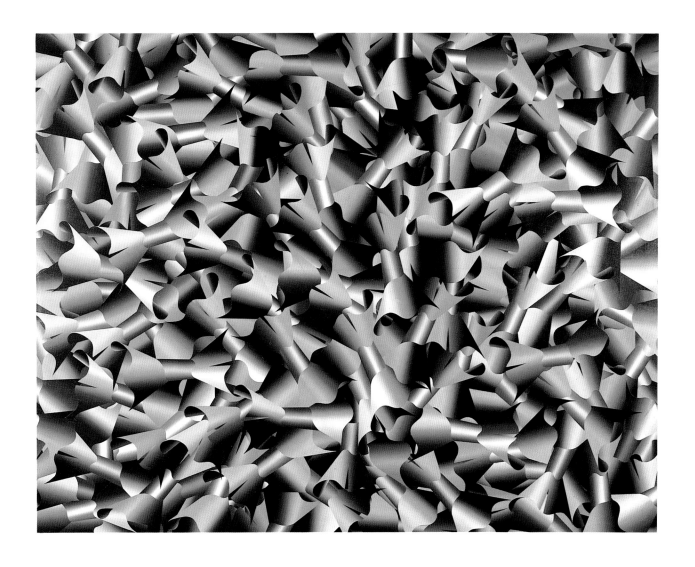

Cat.11

Cat.12

Cat.13

Cat.14

Cat.15

Cat.16

Cat.17

Cat.18

Cat.19

Cat.20

Cat.21

Cat.22

Cat.23

Cat.24

Cat.25

Cat.28

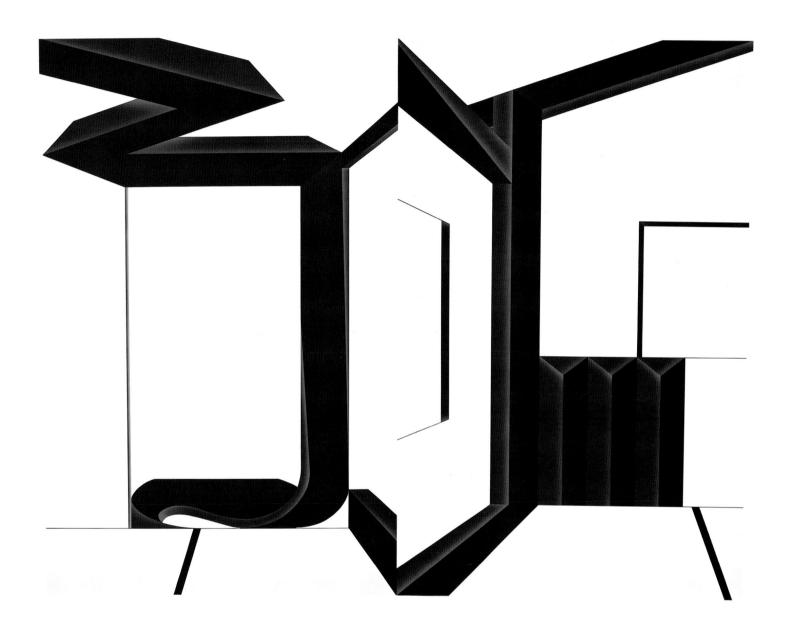

Cat.29

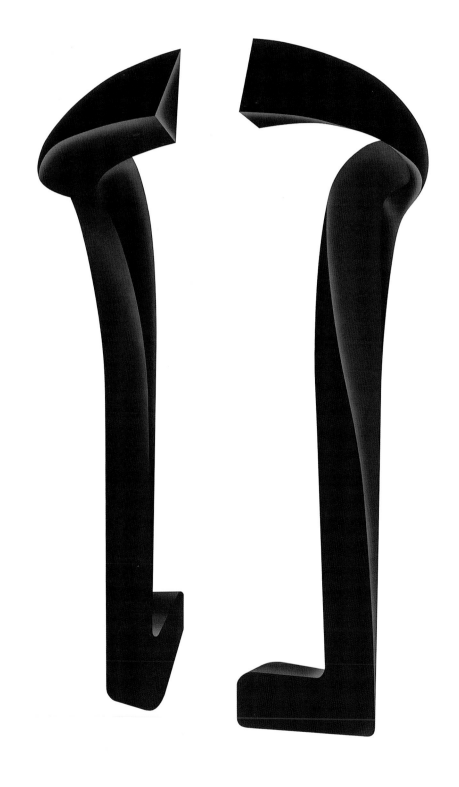

Cat.30

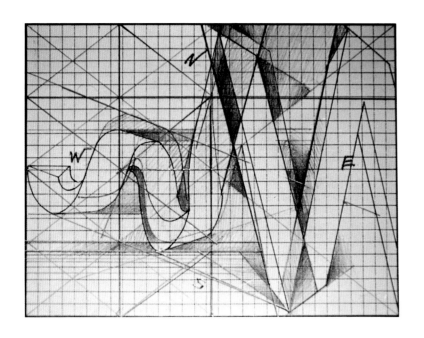

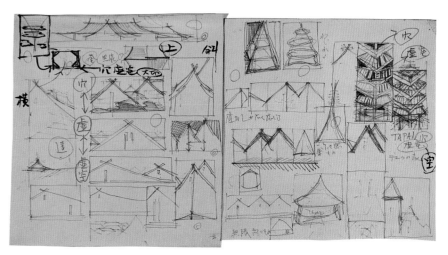

Cat.31

Cat.32

Cat.27

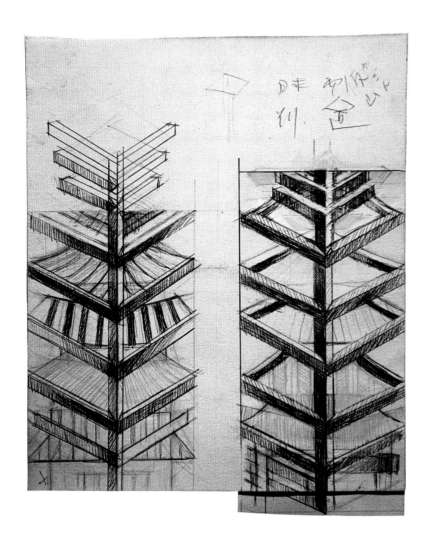

Cat.33

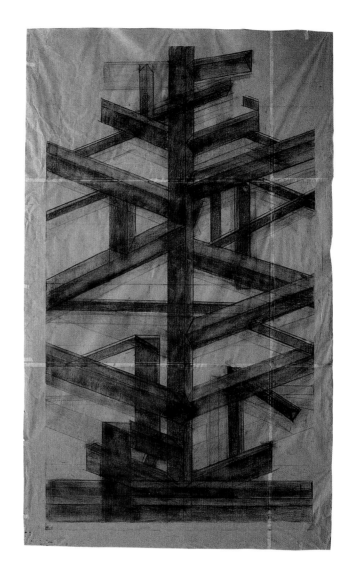

Cat.34

RYU : The Sound of the Wind Blowing from a Distance

Members of Ryu

Akira Miyauchi
Akira Yamasaki
Akiyo Kobayashi
Atsushi Yamaberi
Eiji Saito
Emiko Hayama
Fumie Matsushita
Fumiyo Akiyama
Hideki Imoto
Hidenao Jufuku
Hiroko Tanikawa
Hiroshi Tanikawa
Hisako Shiota
Hitomi Ozaki
Kazuko Hayama
Kazunori Furutake
Kazuyo Hosokawa
Keisei Suzuki
Kenji Kameyama
Kenji Matsumoto
Kenji Takashima
Kimiharu Kato
Koichiro Nishikado
Koji Maruo
Koji Miyoshi
Koji Uemura
Kotoe Moriya
Mari Miyoshi
Masahiko Kikuni
Michihiro Onishi
Michiko Aikawa
Michiko Shioiri
Mika Shinohara
Morikazu Furukawa
Motosi Otsuka
Naotaka Tanimoto
Nobuko Hamano
Noriaki Sangawa
Sanae Kawata
Sanae Kondo
Sawako Kubo
Seiichiro Miike
Shinji Kono
Sumiyo Kondo

Tae Inokuma
Takayuki Nagai
Taku Sakuragi
Tamami Goda
Teruhiro Ando
Tetsuya Tokumaru
Toshihiro Inoue
Tsukasa Kawata
Yoshii Akai
Yoshimi Onishi
Yoshishige Yamaguchi
Yuko Terai

Friends of Ryu

Fumitaka Onishi
Hajime Morita
Kazuyuki Fuke
Kiyoshi Goto
Kunio Nishikado
Masataka Kamada
Masatoshi Hosotani
Masatsuyo Yoshida
Masayuki Hirai
Masayuki Onishi
Masutaka Tanikawa
Nagayoshi Ikeda
Sachiko Ikeda
Shigeyuki Maeda
Takafumi Miyauchi
Takao Kono
Teruko Nagai
Toshiaki Matsuura
Tokio Kawahara
Yasuji Mitani
Yoshiko Matsumoto
Yoshinori Furutake
Yoshio Sakane
Yuzuru Ishibashi

History of Ryu

1971 Toshihiro Hamano established contemporary art group *Ryu* in Sakaide City. At that time there were no local artists tackling contemporary art, so Hamano, who was concerned about the future of contemporary art in the region, decided to mount a campaign to promote the local art culture with several of his pupils.

1972 First year of the annual Ryu Contemporary Art Exhibition, held under the sponsorship of Kagawa Prefecture and Sakaide City.

1973 With the sponsorship of the prefectural board of education, Mr Hamano held summer art classes for children as a means of spreading contemporary art throughout the community.
Educational circles paid great attention to these classes, for they gave children the opportunity to gain an insight into a form of art not able to be covered in the school education curriculum. These classes have continued every year since then, and up to 1991, a total of 5,000 children had taken part in the programme. Fig.14

1977 Art academies were established at various centres in Kagawa Prefecture. The academies were aimed at young workers, and provided lessons in oil painting, print-making, ceramic art, and Indian ink paintings.

1978 At the request of Sakaide City, Hamano jointly produced the stone monument "Ai no To" (Tower of Love) which weights 33 tonnes.

1979 The Gallery Tableau 5 was opened in Sakaide City. This was the first contemporary art gallery in Kagawa Prefecture, and its 210 m² area was used not only for art display, but also for Symposia . The gallery drew national attention, and its opening led to the later establishment of the

Sakaide Art Museun. Fig.15

1980 The Ryu Appreciation society was established, and the then mayor of Sakaide, Mr Tatsuo Banjo, was appointed its first chairman.

Fig.14   Ryu Summer Art School for children

1981 The 21st Century International Exchange Art College was opened in Sakaide City with the aim of promoting international art exchanges and fostering artists. Since then, this has been the headquarters of *Ryu*.

1983 A member of *Ryu* became the first Japanese to attend the Ljubljana Academy of Fine Arts. Since then, with assistance from the Government of Slovenia and the Ljubljana Academy of Fine Arts, *Ryu* has regularly sent students to the academy.

Fig.15   Gallery Tableau 5

1984 The first overseas exhibition of *Ryu* contemporary art was held in the Ljubljana Moderna galerija, under the planning of the gallery director, Dr Zoran Kržišnik.

1985 *Ryu* received the Shikoku Shinbun Cultural Award (Ryu Contemporary Art Group, Representative - Toshihiro Hamano) in recognition of the group's cultural activities both in Japan and overseas and their wide-ranging artistic activities deeply rooted in regional society as they search for contemporary art potentialities. A lecture was held to commemorate the award: guest speaker was the art critic Mr Ichiro Hariu.
Gallery Tableau Mugen (60 ㎡) was opened in Takamatsu City. To mark the gallery's opening, Mr Taro Okamoto gave a commemorative lecture and an exhibition of his work was held. Fig.16
The second overseas exhibition of *Ryu* contemporary art was held, in turn, in three museums: Moderna galerija, Ljubljana and Kärtner Landesgalerie and Wien Palais Palffy in Austria.
The Sakaide Art Museum was opened and Toshihiro Hamano was appointed chairman of the steering committee.
Thirty-four members of *Ryu* displayed work at an exhibition to commemorate the museum's opening.

Fig.16 Gallery Tableau ∞ Mugen

1986 With the cooperation of the Moderna galerija, Ljubljana, exhibitions by contemporary artists from Slovenia were held in Sakaide City, Takamatsu City and Tokyo. For one of the exhibitors, Andrej Jemec, this was the first visit to Japan, and he held a public demonstration of his work at the Gallery Tableau Mugen. Fig.17

Fig.17 Andrej Jemec in Gallery Tableau ∞ Mugen

1987 The exhibition "Hamano & Ryu" was held in the Sakaide Art Museum to support and promote the Kagawa Art Festival.

1988 The director of the Kunsthalle Nürnberg Kunsthalle, Dr Curt Heigl, visited Japan to gather material on "Hamano & Ryu". Dr Heigl gave a presentation entitled "The History of Drawing" at Gallery Tableau Mugen.
Gallery Space Sakaide (81 ㎡) was opened in Sakaide City.
The exhibition International Biennial of Graphic Art Ljubljana in Japan was held in the Sakaide Art Museum and the Kawasaki City Museum. This was the first time that the Ljubljana biennial exhibition had been held in a foreign country, and 109 artists from 18 countries, including successive award winners Joe Tilson and Victor Pasmore from the United Kingdom, exhibited their works. Fig.18
"Hamano & Ryu" was held in the Moderna Galerija, Ljubljana, Kunsthalle Nürnberg , Japanishes Kurturinstitut,

Fig.18 Ljubljana International Biennial of Graphic Art in
Sakaide Art Museum

Fig.19 Hamano with Duncan Macmillan in Gallery
Space Sakaide

Köln, to support and promote the
Japan Foundation.

1989   Sakaide Mayor, Mr Toshiaki Matsuura,
was appointed chairman of the Ryu
Appreciation Society.
A special convention of the Academy
of Comparative Philosophy (chaired by
Dr Hideo Mineshima) was held in
Sakaide City.The convention was
opened with a special presentation by
Dr Hajime Nakamura (recipient of the
Order of Cultural Merits).

1990   The living national treasure Sengoro
Shigeyama gave a performance of a
traditional Noh farce.

1991   At the request of Kagawa Prefecture,
Hamano produced the sculpture for
the Ryokei Bridge in Sakaide and the
Hotarumi Bridge in Mannoucho as
public monuments.
The British Committee for the Japan
Festival 1991 sent Dr Duncan
Macmillan to Japan to gather
information on "Hamano & Ryu". Dr
Macmillan gave a presentation entitled
"The History of Scottish Art" in the
Gallery Tableau Mugen.
In the contemporary art division of
Japan Festival 1991, "Zen: Hamano &
Ryu" opened in Edinburgh and
Sunderland, with assistance from the
Japan Foundation and the Kagawa
Foundation.

Catalogue of Works by Members of Ryu

Akira Miyauchi

Born 1956, Sakaide, Kagawa
1975- Member of *Ryu*
1975-79 Tama Art University, Tokyo
1983-84 Academy of Fine Arts, Ljubljana
Lives and works in Sakaide

One-Person Exhibitions

1979 Tableau 5 Gallery, Sakaide
Osaka Prefectural Contemporary Art
Centre, Osaka
1986 Kunugi Gallery, Tokyo; Tableau 5
Gallery, Sakaide
1987 Kunugi Gallery, Tokyo; Tableau 5
Gallery, Sakaide
1988 Kunugi Gallery, Tokyo
1989 Kunugi Gallery, Tokyo; Space
Sakaide, Sakaide
1990 Kunugi Gallery, Tokyo; Space
Sakaide, Sakaide
1991 Kunugi Gallery, Tokyo; Space
Sakaide, Sakaide

Selected Group Exhibitions

1975-83 Ryu Annual Contemporary Art
Exhibition, Kagawa Prefectural
Culture Hall, Takamatsu
1984 Ryu-razstava, Moderna galerija,
Ljubljana
1985 Ryu International Exhibition, Kagawa
Prefectural Culture Hall, Takamatsu
(also traveled to Kurashiki City
Museum, Okayama; Moderna
galerija, Ljubljana, Yugoslavia;
Kärntner Landesgalerie, Klagenfurt;
Palais Palffy, Wien, Austria)
1986 Sakaide Art Museum: Opening
Exhibition
1987 10 Japanese Artists, Republiški komite
za kulturo SR Slovenije, Ljubljana
New Area: Contemporary Artists in
Shikoku, Prifectural Culture Centre,
Kochi and Tokushima
The 17th International Biennial of

Graphic Art, Moderna galerija,
Ljubljana
Toshihiro Hamano and Artists of Ryu,
Sakaide Art Museum, Sakaide
1988 Hamano and Ryu, Kunsthalle
Nürnberg, Germany (also traveled to
Japanischies Kurturinstitut, Köln;
Moderna galerija, Ljubljana, 1989)
New Area, Ehime Prefectural Culture
Centre, Matsuyama
International Biennial of Graphic
Art Ljbljana in Japan, Sakaide Art
Museum (also traveled to Kawasaki
Art Museum, 1989)
1989 The 18th International Biennial of
Graphic Art, Moderna galerija,
Ljubljana
1990 New Area, Sakaide Art Museum
Sakaide

Cat.35
Water fields 91-1 1991
acrylic on canvas
162.0 × 260.6cm

Cat.35

Eiji Saito

Born 1955, Marugame, Kagawa
1974-   Member of *Ryu*
1974-78 Tama Art University, Tokyo
Lives and works in Marugame

One-Person Exhibitions

1980   Kunugi Gallery, Tokyo; Tableau 5
        Gallery, Sakaide
1981   Kunugi Gallery, Tokyo; Tableau 5
        Gallery, Sakaide
1986   Kunugi Gallery, Tokyo; Tableau 5
        Gallery, Sakaide

Selected Group Exhibitions

1974-83 Ryu Annual Contemporary Art
        Exhibition, Kagawa Prefectural
        Culture Hall, Takamatsu
1984   Ryu-razstava, Moderna galerija,
        Ljubljana
1985   Ryu International Art Exhibition,
        Kagawa Prefectural Culture Hall,
        Takamatsu (also traveled to Kurashiki
        City Museum, Okayama; Moderna
        galerija, Ljubljana, Yugoslavia;
        Kärntner Landesgalerie, Klagenfurt;
        Palais Palffy, Wien, Austria)
        The 2nd International Biennial of
        Graphic Art, CABO-FRIO, Brasil (He
        was awarded the honarary prize)
        Han-Setouchi Contemporary Art
        Exhibition, Okayama Prefectural
        Culture Centre, Okayama
1986   The 9th Japan Emba Annual, Emba
        Art Museum, Ashiya, Kobe
        The 1st Kagawa Biennial, Kagawa
        Prefectural Culture Hall, Takamatsu
        Sakaide Art Museum: Opening
        exhibition
1987   10 Japanese Artists, Republiški komite
        za kulturo SR Slovenije, Ljubjana
        New Area: Contemporary Artists in
        Shikoku, Prefectural Culture Centre,
        Kochi and Tokushima

Toshihiro Hamano and Artists of Ryu,
Sakaide Art Museum, Sakaide
1988   The 4th International Triennial of
        Drawing, Kunsthalle Nürnberg,
        Germany
        New Area, Ehime Prefectural Culture
        Centre, Matsuyama
        From International Exhibitions, Space
        Sakaide
        Hamano and Ryu, Kunsthalle
        Nürnberg, Germany (also traveled to
        Japanischies Kurturinstitut, Köln;
        Moderna galerija, Ljubljana, 1989)
1990   New Area, Sakaide Art Museum
        Sakaide

Cat.36
Space in myself 91-5 1991
Pencil and acrylic on wooden board
160.0×240.0cm

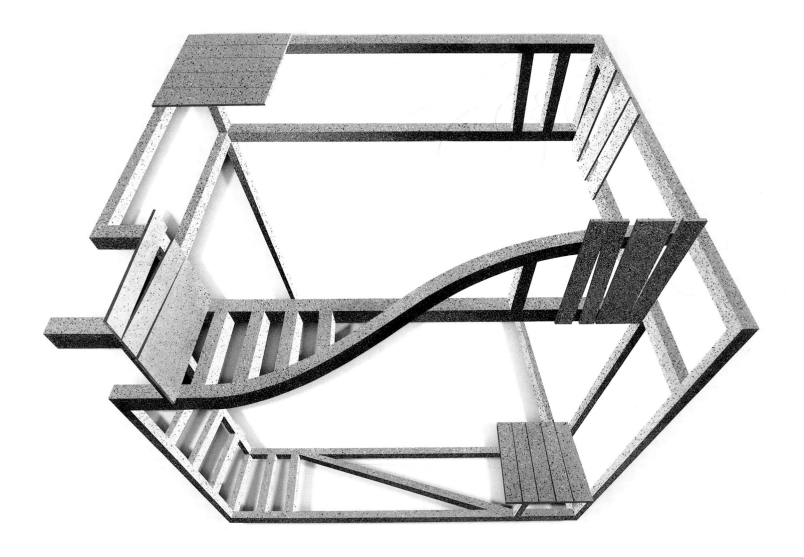

Cat.36

Koji Maruo

Born 1959, Ayauta, Kagawa
1977-   Member of *Ryu*
1977-81 Tama Art University
Lives and works in Ayauta

One-Person Exhibitions

1979   Tableau 5 Gallery, Sakaide
1980   Kunugi Gallery, Tokyo
1981   Kunugi Gallery, Tokyo; Tableau 5
         Gallery, Sakaide
1982   Kunugi Gallery, Tokyo; Tableau 5
         Gallery, Sakaide
1983   Kunugi Gallery, Tokyo; Tableau 5
         Gallery, Sakaide
1984   Tableau 5 Gallery, Sakaide
1985   Kunugi Gallery, Tokyo; Tableau 5
         Gallery, Sakaide
1986   Tableau 5 Gallery, Sakaide
1987   Kunugi Gallery, Tokyo; Tableau 5
         Gallery, Sakaide

Selected Group Exhibition

1977-83 Ryu Annual Contemporary Art
         Exhibition, Kagawa Prefectural
         Culture Hall, Takamatsu
1981   Tableau 5 Gallery: Grand-prix
         Exhibition (He was awarded the
         Grand-prix)
1983   Realism Now, The Museum of
         Modern Art, Saitama, Urawa
         The 6th Japan Emba Annual, Emba
         Art Museum, Ashiya, Kobe
1984   Ryu-razstava, Moderna galerija,
         Ljubljana
1985   Junij: International Art Corection,
         Razstavisce Riharda Jakopica,
         Ljubljana
         Ryu International Art Exhibition,
         Kagawa Prefectural Culture Hall,
         Takamatsu (also traveled to Kurashiki
         City Museum, Okayama; Moderna
         galerija, Ljubljana, Yugoslavia;
         Kärntner Landesgalerie, Klagenfurt;

Palais Palffy, Wien, Austria)
1986   Sakaide Art Museum: Opening
         Exhibition
1987   New Area: Contemporary Artists in
         Shikoku, Prefectural Culture Centre,
         Kochi and Tokushima
         Toshihiro Hamano and Artists of Ryu,
         Sakaide Art Museum, Sakaide
1988   Hamano and Ryu, Kunsthalle
         Nürnberg, Germany (also traveled to
         Japanischies Kurturinstitut, Köln;
         Moderna galerija, Ljubljana, 1989)
         New Area, Ehime Prefectural Culture
         Centre, Matsuyama
1990   New Area, Sakaide Art Museum
         Sakaide

Cat.37
Katsu 1991
acrylic and charcoal on cloth
210.0×300.0cm

Cat.37

Koji Miyoshi

Born 1956, Sakaide, Kagawa
1975-   Member of *Ryu*
1975-79 Tama Art University, Tokyo
1985-86 Academy of Fine Arts, Ljubljana
Lives and works in Sakaide

One-Person Exhibitions

1979   Tableau 5 Gallery, Sakaide
        Osaka Prefectural Contemporary Art
        Centre, Osaka
1981   Gallery Yo, Tokyo; Tableau 5
        Gallery, Sakaide
1982   Kunugi Gallery, Tokyo; Tableau 5
        Gallery, Sakaide
1983   Kunugi Gallery, Tokyo; Tableau 5
        Gallery, Sakaide
1984   Kunugi Gallery, Tokyo; Tableau 5
        Gallery, Sakaide

Selected Group Exhibitions

1975-83 Ryu Annual Contemporary Art
         Exhibition, Kagawa Prefectural
         Culture Hall, Takamatsu
1984   Ryu-razstava, Moderna galerija,
        Ljubljana
1985   Ryu International Art Exhibition,
        Kagawa Prefectural Culture Hall,
        Takamatsu (also traveled to Kurashiki
        City Museum, Okayama; Moderna
        galerija, Ljubljana, Yugoslavia;
        Kärntner Landesgalerie, Klagenfurt;
        Palais Palffy, Wien, Austria)
1986   Sakaide Art Museum: Opening
        Exhibition
1987   10 Japanese Artists, Republiški komite
        za kulturo SR Slovenije, Ljubljana
        New Area:Contemporary Artists in
        shikoku, Prefectural Culture Centre,
        Kochi and Tokushima
        The 17th International Biennial of
        graphic Art, Moderna galerija,
        Ljubljana
        Toshihiro Hamano and Artists of Ryu,

1988   Sakaide Art Museum, Sakaide
        Hamano and Ryu, Kunsthalle
        Nürnberg, Germany (also traveled to
        Japanischies Kurturinstitut, Köln;
        Moderna galerija, Ljubljana, 1989)
        New Area, Ehime Prefectural Culture
        Centre, Matsuyama International
        Biennial of Graphic Art Ljubljana in
        Japan, Sakaide Art Museum (also
        traveled to Kawasaki Art Museum,
        1989)
1989   The 18th International Biennial of
        Graphic Art, Moderna galerija,
        Ljubljana
1990   New Area, Sakaide Art Museum
        Sakaide
        Three Artists, Space Sakaide

Cat.38
Percussion-A 1991
acrylic, crayon and pencil on canvas
181.8×227.3cm

Cat.38

Michihiro Onishi

Born 1964, Kawanoe, Ehime
1983-   Member of *Ryu*
1983-87 Tama Art University, Tokyo
1987-90 Academy of Fine Arts, Ljubljana
lives and works in Ljubljana and Nürnberg

Selected group Exhibitions

1984   Kai, Tableau 5 Gallery, Sakaide
1985   Ryu International Art Exhibition,
        Kagawa Prefectural Culture Hall,
        Takamatsu (also traveled to Kurashiki
        City Museum, Okayama; Moderna
        galerija, Ljubljana, Yugoslavia;
        Kärntner Landesgalerie, Klagenfurt;
        Palais Palffy, Wien, Austria)
1988   Hamano and Ryu, Kunsthalle
        Nürnberg, Germany (also traveled to
        Japanischies Kurturinstitut, Köln;
        Moderna galerija, Ljubljana, 1989)
        New Area, Ehime Prefectural Culture
        Centre,Matsuyama
1989   The 18th International Biennial of
        Graphic Art, Moderna galerija,
        Ljubljana
        Exhibition with T. Ando, Space
        Sakaide, Sakaide
1991   Ustvarjalci Skupine Ryu, Galerija
        Kompas, Ljubljana

Cat.39
Self-III 1991
acrylic and pencil on paper
65.0 × 50.0cm

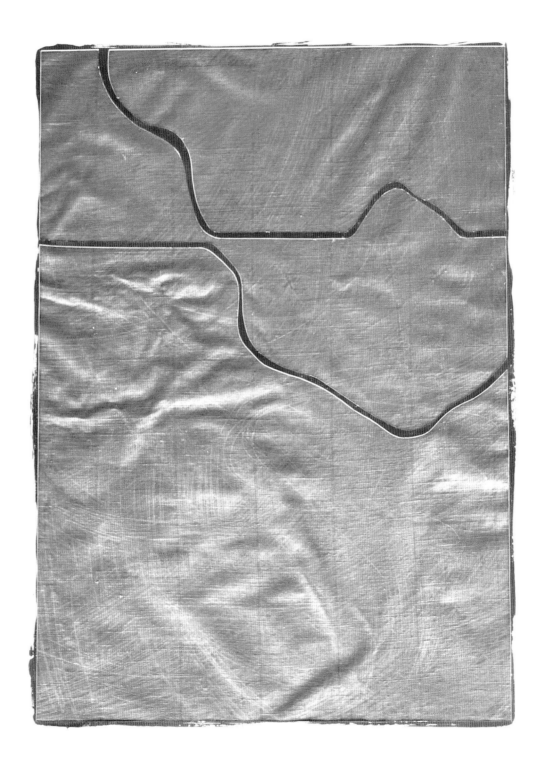

Cat.39

Teruhiro Ando

Born 1962, Zentsuji, Kagawa
1980 Member of *Ryu*
1980-84 Tama Art University, Tokyo
1985-90 Academy of Fine Arts, Ljubljana
lives and works in Edinburgh and Madrid

One-Person Exhibitions

1981 Tableau 5 Gallery, Sakaide
1982 Tableau 5 Gallery, Sakaide
1984 Tableau 5 Gallery, Sakaide
1988 Galerija Ars, Ljubljana
1989 Mala Galerija-Moderna Galerija,
    Ljubljana

Selected Group Exhibitions

1980-83 Ryu Annual Contemporary Art
    Exhibition, Kagawa Prefectural
    Culture Hall, Takamatsu
1984 Third force and We, Tokyo
    Metropolitan Museum
    Ryu - razstava, Moderna galerija,
    Ljubljana
1985 Ryu International Art Exhibition,
    Kagawa Prefectural Culture Hall,
    Takamatsu (also traveled to Kurashiki
    City Museum, Okayama; Moderna
    galerija, Ljubljana, Yugoslavia;
    Kärntner Landesgalerie, Klagenfurt;
    Palais Palffy, Wien, Austria)
1987 10 Japanese Artists, Republiški komite
    za kulturo SR Slovenije, Ljubljana
    The 17th International Biennial of
    Graphic Art, Moderna galerija,
    Ljubljana
1988 The 11th International Biennial of
    Original Drawings, Moderna
    galerija, Rijeka
    Razstava likovnih del ALU, Musej
    revolucije, Celje
    Hamano and Ryu, Kunsthalle
    Nürnberg, Germany (also traveled to
    Japanischies Kurturinstitut, Köln;
    Moderna galerija, Ljubljana, 1989)

International Biennial of Graphic Art
Ljubljana, in Japan, Sakaide Art
Museum (also traveled to Kawasaki
Art Museum, 1989)
1989 The 18th International Biennial of
    Graphic Art, Moderna galerija,
    Ljubljana
    Exhibition with M. Onishi, Space
    Sakaide
1991 Ustvarjalci Skupine Ryu, Galerija
    Kompas, Ljubljana

Cat.40
Sketch for the project
"Homage to Kukai", A-1, 1991
pencil and crayon on paper
45.0×32.0cm

Cat.41
Sketch for the project
"Homage to Kukai", B-1,2 1991
pencil on paper
60.0×85.0cm

Cat.40

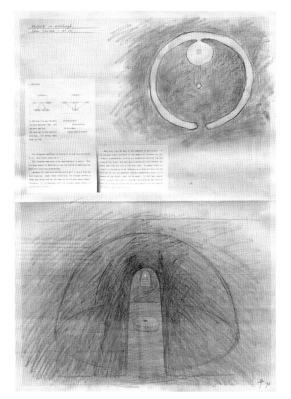

Cat.41

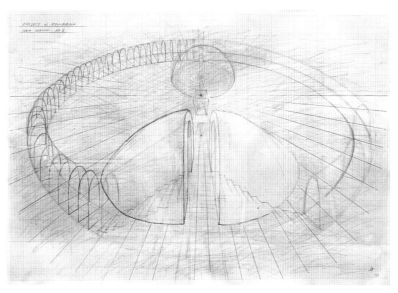

Cat.41

ZEN : HAMANO & RYU

Contemporary Art from Japan

Edited by
Talbot Rice Gallery;
Duncan Macmillan, Bill Hare
NCCA, Sunderland;
Mike Hill
Ryu Contemporary Art
Designed by Talbot Rice Gallery,
Ryu Contemporary Art
Photography by *Hiroshi Tanikawa*
© Ryu Contemporary Art and the authors,
1991
ISBN 0 9503567 8 6